CUBA ⚡

CUBA

CASTRO, REVOLUTION, AND THE END OF THE EMBARGO

LIGHTNING
GUIDES

Front Cover Photo: © Hugh Sitton/CORBIS. Back Cover Photo: Danita Delimont/Gallo Images Interior Photos: Liu Bin/Xinhua/Eyevine/Redux, p.1; Lee Frost/Offset, p.2; Gabriel Tichy/Stocksy, p.5; Public Domain, Wikimedia Commons, p.6; Natalie Grono/Getty Images, p.7; Richard Semik/Shutterstock, p.9; Peter Hermes Furian/Shutterstock, p.9; thaagoon/Shutterstock, p.9; danm12/Shutterstock, p.9; Jan Karel Donatus Van Beecq (1638-1722) [Public domain]/Wikimedia Commons, p.13; DEA PICTURE LIBRARY/Getty Images, p.14; MarcPo/Thinkstock, p.14; Bruce Hallman [Public domain]/Wikimedia Commons, p.17; Robert Van Der Hilst/Getty Images, p.18; Picsfive/Shutterstock, p.20; ittipon/Shutterstock, p.20; Harris & Ewing [Public domain]/Wikimedia Commons, p.23; gmutlu/iStock, p.24; ullstein bild/Getty Images, p.25; Cecil Stoughton, White House [Public domain]/Wikimedia Commons, p.27; FPG/Hulton Archive/Getty Images, p.31; Everett Historical/Shutterstock, p.33; Bettmann/CORBIS, p. 37; Neftali/Shutterstock, p.38; Macdonald-Ross [Public domain]/Wikimedia Commons, p.38; Pictorial Press Ltd/Alamy, p.38; Frans Schellekens/Getty Images, p.38; Photos 12/Alamy, p.38; sjvinyl/Alamy, p.39; ZUMA Press, Inc./Alamy, p.39; DWD-Media/Alamy, p.39; Michael Caulfield/AMA2010/Getty Images, p.39; mchen007/iStock, p.39; Echoes/Getty Images, p.39; Frans Schellekens/Getty Images, p.39; © Sueddeutsche Zeitung Photo/Alamy, p.39; Bettmann/CORBIS, p.41; Alberto Diaz Gutierrez (Alberto Korda) (Museo Che Guevara, Havana, Cuba) [Public domain]/Wikimedia Commons, p.42; Bettmann/CORBIS, p.47; Desmond Boylan/CORBIS, p.48; Neftali/Shutterstock, p.53; Helga Esteb/Shutterstock, p.53; cinemafestival/Shutterstock, p.53; Featureflash/Shutterstock, p.53; © Barry Lewis/Alamy, p.54; © Edward Childs, p.54; Alberto Korda (Museo Che Guevara, Havana Cuba) [Public domain]/Wikimedia Commons, p.56; Getty Images, p.59; Daxus/iStock, p.64; corund/Shutterstock, p.64; VanHart/Shutterstock, p.64; Margo Harrison/Shutterstock, p.65; Nagel Photography/Shutterstock, p.65; Public Domain/Wikimedia Commons, p.65; Everett Historical/Shutterstock, p.66; Olga Popova/Shutterstock.com, p.66; KeithBinns/iStock, p. 66; Veronica Louro/Shuttersock, p.67; EduardoLuzzatti/iStock, p.67; EdStock/iStock, p.67; Anadolu Agency/Getty Images, p.70; Gilberto Ante/Roger Viollet/Getty Images, p.71; Chris Cheadle/Getty Images, p.73; © Charlotte Thege/Alamy, p.73; © Karolina Webb/Alamy, p.73; sergign/Shutterstock, p.74; PALM/RSCH/Getty Images, p.76; Eric Cabanis/Getty Images, p.77; ASSOCIATED PRESS, p.78; Jeremy Woodhouse/Getty Images, p.79; © Roberto Fumagalli/Alamy, p.81; © Jeff Greenberg 6 of 6/Alamy, p.82; r.classen/Shutterstock, p.83; Sean Pavone/Shutterstock, p.86,87; © imagestock/iStock, p.89; Hang Dinh/Shutterstock, p91;blackred/iStock, p.93; stockphoto-graf/Shutterstock, p.96; Universal History Archive/GettyImages, p.97; Roberto A Sanchez/Getty Images, p.100; Featureflash/Shutterstock, p.103; © Annette Lozinski/Alamy, p.106

"Mountains culminate in peaks, and nations in men."
—JOSÉ MARTÍ

What do we imagine when we speak of Cuba? Nestled like a jewel among the glittering waters of the Caribbean, it has been home to mobsters and poets, artists and revolutionaries. It is a fixture in the American imagination, a place of legend and mystery, of crushing poverty and unfettered spirit. Its troubled and codependent relationship with the United States has made it eternally relevant, and now, as America prepares to relax its embargo, Cuba, once more, is calling. "Hasta la victoria, sempre," wrote Che Guevara, departing to carry the revolution to the Congo and later Bolivia, where he would be captured and killed. And today, indeed, the battle is not yet won as Cuba searches for its freedom, its identity, and its future.

CONTENTS

INTRODUCTION

hen Christopher Columbus first set foot in Cuba, in 1492, he described it as "the most beautiful earth that human eyes have seen." His marvel at the physical beauty was fully justified. Cuba was an unspoiled vista of natural beauty that boasted thousands of plant species, trees, and flowers as well as hundreds of tropical birds that fluttered above the grasslands punctuated by palm trees, yucca, and pineapple.

Impressions of Cuba today could hardly be more different. Many people think of Cuba as an isolated nation where time has reputedly stood still since the 1950s, or as the center of political unrest in the Caribbean region under the iron hand of a single-party state led by a family of dictators. The island has become famous for its music, cigars, literature, and vintage automobiles. But these iconic images have a way of obscuring what really goes on in a country that has long been separated from its neighbors and the wider world.

After taking office in 2008, President Raúl Castro diminished Cuba's adherence to a socialist agenda and initiated economic reforms. Starting in 2014, the United States has been attempting to normalize diplomatic relations between the two nations. Slowly the Cuban economy is gaining access to foreign commerce and travel. Soon, more visitors will be able to see what enchanted Christopher Columbus about Cuba.

As Cuba returns to the world stage, our old impressions of it will no longer suffice. The future of the western hemisphere depends, in part, on what emerges from this famously isolated and misunderstood island.

Havana is often referred to as **THE ROME OF THE CARIBBEAN**

CUBA IS HOME *to just over* **11 MILLION PEOPLE**

CUBA IS THE LARGEST ISLAND *IN THE CARRIBBEAN ISLES,* sitting independently in an archipelago in the **NORTH CARIBBEAN SEA**

2.1 *MILLION PEOPLE LIVE IN* **HAVANA**

POPE JOHN PAUL II VISITED THE ISLAND IN **1998** becoming the **FIRST PONTIFF** to make an official visit

Who is Elián González?

In November 1999, five-year-old Elián González made global headlines when he was discovered in the sea between Cuba and Florida, one of a few survivors of a group of refugees attempting to sail to the United States. A long custody battle between González's father in Cuba and relatives in Florida strained already tense relations between Cuba and the United States, but it ended when American federal agents forcibly removed González from his relatives' Florida home. Accompanied by his father, Elian returned to Cuba in June 2000.

Why did relations with the rest of the world deteriorate?

After decades of unrest and revolution, the socialist leader Fidel Castrowho legalized the Communist Party, eventually seized control of Cuba. In 1960, he signed commercial agreements with the Soviet Union, which led to President Eisenhower laying plans to overthrow the Castro regime. Carried out by Eisenhower's successor, John F. Kennedy, the failure of the maneuvers and the subsequent missile crisis led to a freezing of all diplomatic relations.

What is the healthcare system in Cuba?

Cuba reputedly has one of the world's most comprehensive primary-care programs. All health services are provided free of charge at the point of treatment. Cuba boasts the lowest infant mortality rate in Latin America.

Can I travel to Cuba?

The longstanding ban on Americans traveling to the island nation has been amended to permit US citizens to participate in tours that encourage "people-to-people" contact. Prior to this recent change, Americans could still visit as part of educational, cultural, or religious groups approved by the Department of State. Americans still need to travel with an organization officially approved by the US State Department.

What is the currency of Cuba?

Cuba operates a dual-currency system, though the government has announced plans to simplify to having one currency in the future. Cuban convertible pesos (CUC) are used for the tourist economy and are set at an exchange level with the US dollar. Local wages and prices are set in Cuban pesos (CUP). Rationing of food and other staples is in place for locals, who use a monthly ration book for supplies.

What are the main industries in Cuba?

Cuba built its economy during Spanish rule by exporting tobacco and sugarcane. These remain vital to the economic well-being of the country. However, nickel, coffee, and rum are also key industries. Perhaps surprisingly, tourism may be the most important industry to the economy. Still, biotech and pharmaceutical research and production are beginning to prosper.

What was the Bay of Pigs incident?

In April 1961, the CIA executed a military campaign to topple Cuba's revolutionary government. The invasion was carried out by Brigade 2506, a paramilitary group of Cuban exiles who landed at Playa Girón from Guatemala. The invasion failed, the brigade surrendered, and its members were sent to the US after public interrogations. The invasion had the unwanted effect of building popular support for the Cuban government.

What triggered the Cuban missile crisis?
In 1962, the Cuban missile crisis brought the world to the brink of nuclear war, with American president John F. Kennedy poised to launch missiles in response to Soviet plans to build a nuclear weapons base on the island. Eventually, the standoff ended with the Soviet Union withdrawing the missiles in return for the United States promising not to invade Cuba.

Why does the United States maintain a military base at Guantánamo Bay?
The newly formed Republic of Cuba leased 45 square miles of land in Guantánamo Bay to the United States for construction of a naval station, just a few years after the Treaty of Paris had ended Spain's rule. Building on the naval station began in 1903, and the station remains occupied by the United States more than a century later. Although the United States pays a leasing fee for the land, Cuba has not accepted payment since the Cuban Revolution.

What is Cuba's international future?
In 2014, President Barack Obama announced plans to normalize diplomatic relations and ease economic restrictions on Cuba, a policy shift he called the end of an "outdated approach" to US-Cuban relations that, "for decades, has failed to advance our interests." Obama has promised to initiate moves toward reopening the US embassy in Havana and allowing some travel and trade that had long been banned under the embargo that was first imposed during the Kennedy administration.

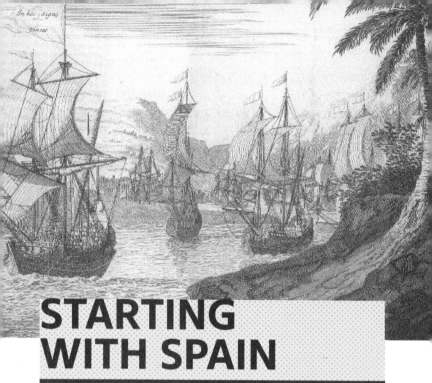

STARTING WITH SPAIN

THE COLONIZATION OF CUBA

On October 28, 1492, Christopher Columbus landed on the shores of Bariay on the northeastern coast of Cuba (then called Coabana). His fleet was comprised of three ships—La Pinta, La Nina, and La Santa Maria. Upon docking, Columbus declared the island as "Isla Juana," after the Asturian Prince Juan, claiming it for the Kingdom of Spain.

DID YOU KNOW

Columbus sailed from San Salvador using navigation routes given to him by the natives. When he spotted Cuba he was convinced he had arrived in East Asia and that the island was the coast of China.

Until Columbus' arrival, Cuba was inhabited by indigenous people known as the Taino (also called the Arawak) and the Ciboney. The Ciboney were migrants who had driven out the earlier Guanajatabey inhabitants. While the Ciboney were mainly hunters and fishers, the Taíno were primarily farmers.

In 1494 shortly after Pope Alexander VI had commanded Spain to conquer, colonize, and convert all the pagan natives to Catholicism, Columbus returned to the island, this time sailing through the south coast waters of the island, and landing at many of the bays along the rocky coastline. In 1494—shortly after Pope Alexander VI had commanded Spain to conquer, colonize, and convert all the pagan natives to Catholicism—Columbus returned to the island, this time sailing through the south coast waters of the island, and

Even before the Spanish conquest, the indigenous tribes were under threat from other invaders, including the Caribs, cannibalistic warriors sailing north from South America. Although they never settled on the island, the Caribs terrorized the Taíno and the Ciboney, periodically landing and raiding their villages.

landing at many of the bays along the rocky coastline. Through Columbus, Spain focused most of its attention on the larger Hispaniola island (home to Haiti and the Dominican Republic). It wasn't until 1509 that Cuba was fully mapped. The completion of this task by Sebastián de Ocampo enabled Diego Velázquez de Cuéllar to form the first Spanish settlement in Cuba, which was founded at Baracoa in 1511.

Thousands of peaceful tribal villagers who greeted the Spanish with food and supplies were, in return, butchered without provocation. The Taíno tribes, some of whose leaders escaped to Cuba from the brutal Spanish regime on Hispaniola, fought a bloody resistance.

This resistance lasted three years until the Spanish gained control and, in 1514, Havana was settled.

A measles and smallpox epidemic, which began in 1529, contributed further to the decimation of the native population. In 1550, the diminished native population was given freedom to establish their own townships, particularly in eastern Cuba, where their descendants survive today.

Unlike many of the Caribbean plantation islands, Cuba has been mainly reliant on a diverse agricultural economy. As the British and French used slave labor culled from the indigenous populace to develop the islands they colonized, so Cuba's Spanish rulers developed a more urban society by enslaving no fewer than 50,000 Cuban men and women.

JOSÉ MARTÍ

THE APOSTLE OF CUBAN INDEPENDENCE AND THE STRUGGLE FOR DEMOCRACY

Although José Julian Martí Perez lived a short life, dying at 42 years old, his influence on Cuba's struggle for democracy was such that he became known as the Apostle of Cuban Independence.

Born in Havana in 1853, Martí spent much of his early life traveling throughout Latin America, the United States, and Spain. During his teenage years, Martí became passionate about the cause of Cuban political and intellectual independence.

While at Madrid University, Martí began to debate and protest Spanish activity in Cuba publicly. After graduating with a degree in canon and civil law, in 1875, Martí left Spain for Calle Moneda, (near Mexico City), where he began publishing his opinions on current political events in José Vicente Villada's Revista Universal. Then, in 1877, he headed to Guatemala where he was commissioned by the government to write Patria y Libertad (Drama Indio).

Martí made the promotion of liberty his lifelong passion, and he was one of the earliest voices raising concerns about

THE FIRST DUTY OF A MAN IS TO THINK FOR HIMSELF —JOSÉ MARTÍ

American expansionism within Cuba. He was also a very outspoken critic of slavery and Spain's failure to completely abolish the abhorrent practice.

1894 found Martí in the United States. He became the leading mind behind the expedition that would sail from Florida to begin the revolution. The expedition landed at Playitas on April 11, 1895. The rebellion was not a success. Local support had been woefully misjudged and did not materialize. Little more than a month after landing on Cuban soil, the revolutionaries faced off against Spanish troops at the Battle of Dos Ríos, and Martí was killed. The fighting continued with varying degrees of success and failure, many admitted Martí's death was a huge blow to the cause.

His thoughts on Cuban and Latin American sovereignty continue to shape the modern Latin identity. Martí is often cited by Fidel Castro as the crucial inspiration for his communist government. As a result, Martí's writings are still predominantly featured in the Cuban battle of ideology.

Liberty, democracy, and freedom were recurring themes in his works, and a poem taken from his posthumously published book, *Simple Verses*, became the inspiration for Cuba's patriotic song, "Guantanamera."

HOW SWEET IT ISN'T

HOW SUGAR SHAPED CUBA

Cuba has a proverb that translates as "Without sugar, there's no country." Surprisingly, sugarcane is not indigenous to the island. Diego Velazquez de Cuellar is credited with having introduced the crop sometime in 1511.

Initially, tobacco was the main focus of the Cuban economy as established by Spain. Tobacco farming required enormous amounts of labor, which simply couldn't be fulfilled by the indigenous people. Soon, as was the case in parts of the Caribbean under British and French control, the importation of African slaves began. However, the Spanish slave trade grew at a much slower pace than that of the British and the French.

The growth of the Cuban economy suffered as a result of strict trade laws and its slow-to-start slave importation. British-occupied Barbados and French-controlled Haiti (known then as Saint-Domingue) began to dominate the world's sugarcane growth and processing. But the tide turned for Cuba when Britain occupied the island for a short time from 1762 to 1763, resulting in a massive increase in slave importation. The exponential increase in the number of slaves with expertise in sugar refining, coupled with the perfect conditions for sugar-cane cultivation in Cuba, led to a shift in the island's agricultural focus from tobacco to sugar.

Spain soon recognized that Cuba was the perfect place to harness the world's booming desire for sugar. Technological advances such as furnaces, steam-powered engines, and water mills enabled the Spanish in Cuba to produce a much higher quality of refined sugar. And so, the 19th century saw a boom in the sugar industry on the island. This led to many infrastructure improvements, including the building of railroads to enable the fast transportation of the cane, largely thanks to huge American financial investment by the United Fruit Company. Formed in 1899, United Fruit owned vast tracts of land and infrastructure throughout Central and South America as well as in the Caribbean islands, including sugar mills in Cuba.

The booming sugar industry led to Cuba becoming almost solely devoted to growing cane, at the expense of all other farmed crops and industries. It became vital to import almost all other necessary goods, making Cuba dependent on the United States, the primary importer of Cuban sugar at an 80 percent share. The abolition of slavery in 1886 caused considerable problems for the sugar economy. It also forced planters to resort to illegally buying slave workers, who were far more expensive.

The seemingly never-ending wars of independence further eroded Cuba's dominance of the global sugar industry. Specifically, the Ten Years' War and the War of Independence led to a concentration of growing refineries in the West, as well as in the areas around Havana. This left Cuba's sugar industry vulnerable during the prolonged wars. The sugar industry was primed for an American takeover and the United States gained control of the island under the 1898 Treaty of Paris.

KINGS OF SUGAR

By 1860, there were around 2,000 sugar mills in Cuba, and the output was responsible for about one-third of the world's sugar. This dominance gave rise to Cuba's reputation as "King Sugar."

With the United States in control of the island at the start of the 20th century and the Reciprocity Treaty lowering the US tariff on Cuban sugar by 20 percent, the United Fruit Company began building vast factories and improved processing techniques to further enhance Cuba's status as the "King" of the sugar industry.

The 1959 nationalization of the sugar industry ended the influence of the United Fruit Company, which Castro accused of having aided Cuban exiles and financing a possible invasion by the United States. At the same time, Venezuela-born Julio Lobo, who married into Cuban aristocracy and was the most powerful Cuban sugar financier and trader, left the island to go into exile, relinquishing his vast holdings on the Cuban sugar industry.

The Saint-Domingue rebellion in 1791 wiped out the island's sugar industry at a time when the demand for the product was rising. It was perfect timing for Cuba to shift focus to sugarcane growth and refining.

CANE & COIN : CUBA'S EXPORTS

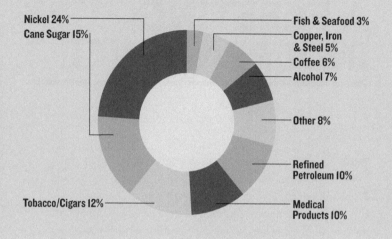

Nickel 24%
Cane Sugar 15%
Fish & Seafood 3%
Copper, Iron & Steel 5%
Coffee 6%
Alcohol 7%
Other 8%
Refined Petroleum 10%
Tobacco/Cigars 12%
Medical Products 10%

Castro's policies led to greater dependence on the sugar harvest over the subsequent decades, with inflated pricing from the Soviet Union, sugar's largest importer at that time. Various crises resulted. Most notably, in 1970, Castro demanded an annual quota of 10 million tons of sugar crops, leading to increased focus on the crop to the exclusion of almost all else. The quota could never be met.

By the 21st century, Cuba's contribution to the world's sugar market had fallen to around 1 percent. Although there were government plans to confine sugar production to a smaller number of mills, increasing the quality of production, this policy failed. In 2012, Brazil-based Odebrecht became the first foreign company permitted to administer sugar mills since the revolution.

A FLEETING INDEPENDENCE

THE ONGOING US-CUBA DANCE

F our years after the 1895 revolution that ended Spanish colonialism, the United States finally ceded control of Cuba to the Cuban government. The transfer came with conditions, which were outlined in the Platt Amendment and incorporated into Cuba's new constitution. One of these provisions empowered the United States to intervene with military force should conditions warrant it.

Cuba's first democratic elections were held in 1902, with former revolutionary Tomás Estrada Palma (who had succeeded Carlos Manuel de Céspedes as leader of the Republic in Arms in 1873) elected the first independent Cuban head of state. He immediately confirmed independence through a declaration.

When Palma sought a second term in office at the end of his four-year presidency, his reelection triggered a new revolt, led by the young and idealistic general Enrique Loynaz del Castillo.

Exercising its right under the constitution to intervene, the US initiated the Cuban Pacification in September 1906, leading to Cuba's second occupation. President Teddy Roosevelt dispatched

{
Colonialism *co·lo·ni·al·ism*
The acquisition, establishment, exploitation, and expansion of a colony in one territory by a political power from another territory.
}

Fulgencio Batista meets General Malin Craig, Chief of Staff of the United States Army, who had invited Batista to the US, and Undersecretary of State Sumner Welles in Washington DC, 1938.

an invasion force that reoccupied the island nation for the next four years. Although he was resented by the Cubans, Roosevelt's main aims were to pacify the fighting between ethnic groups and reinstate free elections. However, he also declared his intent to fully protect American economic investments.

Then-Secretary of War William Howard Taft led the American diplomatic efforts to end Castillo's attempted coup, by pressuring Palma to resign the presidency. Roosevelt subsequently appointed Charles Magoon as the US governor of Cuba,

DID YOU KNOW

Despite Cuba's declaration of independence, the entire island was not under Cuban control. As part of the Platt agreement, Guantánamo Bay was leased to the United States. Isla de la Juventuds was not stipulated as being American territory, but it remained under US control until 1925.

overseeing American control. Elections followed in November 1908, which saw José Miguel Gómez become the second president. Two months later, the United States withdrew its troops and Governor Magoon.

The more liberal Gómez served one term as president from 1908 to 1913 before being defeated by the conservative Mario García Menocal, who was elected twice, resulting in an eight-year presidency, from 1913 to 1921. On April 1917, Cuba joined the United States in declaring war on Germany and played a key role in protecting the Caribbean from incursions from German U-Boats. Although a draft was created and 25,000 Cuban troops were called up to join the American forces in Europe, the war ended before they were deployed.

Menocal, a former executive within the Cuban American Sugar Corporation, saw income from sugar rise dramatically during his first term in office. After his 1916 reelection, the former President Gómez attempted an armed coup to

[**During Magoon's** governorship, the Cuban Communist Party was founded by Agustín Martin Veloz and Francisco Rosales.]

regain control of the nation. US Marines promptly arrived, capturing Gómez and quickly diffusing the rebellion.

In 1921, Alfredo Zayas was elected president for just one term and immediately faced a financial crisis following a drop in sugar prices. The Cuban financial system collapsed, leading Zayas to seek a loan from the US government.

Despite the general Cuban misgivings of American intervention, the United States did nothing when the next president, Gerardo Machado, refused to call elections and stand down when his single term of office ended. Elected in 1925, Machado had an expansive vision to forge a more modern Cuba and inaugurated many civil projects, including the construction of the central highway. Determined to fulfill his vision, Machado evolved into a de facto dictator by refusing to stand down, which led to a number of uprisings. But with no American support or any action by the burgeoning Communist Party of Cuba, the uprisings made little impact.

In 1933, a popular rebellion finally ousted Machado, when a number of young academics, students, and soldiers formed a loose coalition to seize power

ALFREDO ZAYAS

Many historians have pointed out that during the financial crisis under Zayas's rule, Cuba was only nominally independent. American financial and military intervention had in fact made Cuba a colony in all regards but name.

and form a provisional revolutionary government. Carlos Manuel de Céspedes briefly took control, only to be ousted by Ramón Grau San Martín, a physician. Grau led the leftist coalition and immediately discarded the Platt Amendment. Sweeping political changes followed his power seizure, which led to the introduction of huge social reforms. A newly created ministry of labor introduced a standard working day and a minimum wage for cane cutters. Additionally, peasants were given land rights for the first time, and quotas were introduced to guarantee Cuban natives at least 50 percent of all jobs available in agriculture. Although Grau's reforms were radical, they were overthrown in January 1934 by another loose collective of antigovernment thinkers and militia. After six years of short-lived rule by a series of puppet presidents, Cubans elected the right-wing Fulgencio Batista y Zaldívar to be their leader in 1940—supported, not coincidentally, by the United States.

THE PRESIDENTS

FROM EISENHOWER TO OBAMA

E leven presidents of the United States of America have sat in the Oval Office since the Cuban Revolution brought Fidel Castro to power and communism took control of the island. Each president faced challenges in regard to US-Cuban relations.

The Executive Committee of the National Security Council meeting in October 1962, in the Cabinet Room, White House.

DWIGHT D. EISENHOWER (R) PRESIDENT 1953–1961

Eisenhower was in office during the Cuban Revolution, which saw the overthrow of the corrupt dictator Fulgencio Batista. Eisenhower officially recognized the Castro-led Cuban government that followed. Fearing the increasing communist influence, Eisenhower implemented stronger trade restrictions that had devastating effects on the Cuban economy. When Cuba expelled US diplomats, Eisenhower moved to close the American embassy in Havana.

JOHN F. KENNEDY (D) PRESIDENT 1961–1963

Highly critical of Eisenhower's policies, Kennedy publicly vowed to reverse overt American influence at the expense of Cuban liberty, but privately approved a CIA-led armed invasion of the Bay of Pigs in 1961, which was repelled by Cuban forces. Kennedy banned all but humanitarian trade and imposed a travel ban for Americans following the discovery of Soviet missile bases in Cuba.

LYNDON B. JOHNSON (D) PRESIDENT 1963–1969

Tense relations thawed under Johnson's presidency, encouraged by diplomatic overtures from Castro. Despite this, under Johnson's watch, the CIA made further attempts to assassinate the Cuban leader, allegedly even attempting to poison his boot polish.

RICHARD M. NIXON (R) PRESIDENT 1969–1974

A series of hijackings in airspace between the United States and Cuba by citizens of both nations led to increased dialogue and cooperation under Nixon. In 1974, the first US officials since the Eisenhower era visited the island.

GERALD R. FORD (R) PRESIDENT 1974–1977

Ford discovered that Cuba had deployed more than 30,000 troops
to Angola, a nation already supported by the Soviet Union.
Although Ford successfully lobbied to exclude Angola from the
United Nations after Angola's declaration of independence in
1975, he was prevented by Congress from taking any military
action against the African nation.

JAMES E. CARTER (D) PRESIDENT 1977–1981

The Carter administration formulated the Maritime Boundary
Treaty in 1977, which established the location of the border
between Cuba and Florida. Under his presidency, both the US
and Cuba opened interests in each of their respective capital
cities. Castro allowed 125,000 Cubans to leave for the United
States toward the end of 1980.

RONALD W. REAGAN (R) PRESIDENT 1981–1989

Reagan tightened the trade embargo with Cuba and extended
the travel ban for American citizens, prohibiting them from
spending any money in the island. The ban also extended to all
Cuban government officials visiting the United States.

GEORGE H. W. BUSH (R) PRESIDENT 1989–1993

In the post–Cold War era, Castro accused Panamanian leader
Manuel Noriega of being an American spy and using Panama to
traffic drugs into the United States. Bush increased humanitarian relief for Cuba post-Soviet collapse, but he signed the Cuban
Democracy Act, which strengthened the US trade embargo.

WILLIAM J. CLINTON (D) PRESIDENT 1993–2001

Bill Clinton enacted the Helms-Burton Democratic Solidarity Act in 1996, which allowed sanctions against non-US companies trading with Cuba. Clinton later took steps to increase cultural exchanges, easing some of the most stringent travel restrictions. A two-game baseball match between the Baltimore Orioles and the national Cuban team took place as a result. Clinton became the first US president to publicly shake Castro's hand at a United Nations meeting.

GEORGE W. BUSH (R) PRESIDENT 2001–2009

The second President Bush tightened travel restrictions again and, following his 2004 reelection, declared Cuba an "outpost of tyranny," accusing its government of maintaining biological weapons. All embargoes were strictly enforced and strengthened, even after the resignation of Fidel Castro in 2008.

BARACK OBAMA (D) PRESIDENT 2009–PRESENT

Softening language between the two new presidents, Obama and Raúl Castro, led to secret talks brokered in Canada by Pope Francis. A framework for normalizing relations between the two nations was published on December 17, 2014. High-level diplomats from both sides met in Havana in January 2015 to further the relaxation of travel restrictions and discuss new trade deals.

BATISTA

DEMOCRAT TO DICTATOR

IN 1940, Fulgencio Batista y Zaldívar, the self-appointed chief of the armed forces, led Cuba through democratic elections, elevated his position from sergeant to colonel, and effectively took control of the clique that assumed the presidency.

Batista won as the candidate supported by the Democratic Socialist Coalition. His campaign successfully branded his main challenger, the former leader Ramón Grau San Martín, as a fascist. Upon taking office legitimately, Batista adopted the Constitution of 1940, which was regarded as progressive. One of the provisions prevented him from running for office again at the end of his term.

Born in 1901, Batista had a mixed ethnic background, with his father claiming part Chinese heritage. There was some confusion over the registration of his birth, because his mother named him Rubén Zaldívar. He later adopted the name Fulgencio Batista.

[
World War II proved strategically beneficial for Cuba as the first of the Latin American countries to join the global conflict. The island's location made Cuba a key player in protecting the Gulf of Mexico, and its natural resources were very useful to the United States.
]

When he was young, Batista took many different jobs to support himself, including cane cutting, tailoring, working as a mechanic, and selling fruit. In 1921, Batista enlisted as a private in the Cuban army. As part of his basic training, he learned typing and shorthand, which helped him find work teaching stenography when he left the army. He joined the rural police force in 1923, and shortly thereafter, reenlisted in the army. He was soon promoted to the rank of corporal.

By 1933, Batista had infiltrated several revolutionary thinking groups within the military and led them through the uprising that overthrew Gerardo Machado during the brief Revolt of the Sergeants. Replacing Machado and his short-lived successors was Ramón Grau San Martín, who appointed Colonel Batista to head the armed forces as chief of staff. Only 100 days into Grau's presidency, he was ousted by Carlos Mendieta. However, Mendieta's regime only lasted for eleven months. Two equally short-lived leaders then took control: José Barnet, who lasted five months, and Miguel Mariano Góme, who was in power for seven months. Finally, some semblance of continuity was established when Federico Laredo Brú became president in December 1936, and led Cuba for the next four years. In October 1940, President Brú called for free elections, which were won by Colonel Batista.

After being elected, Batista made good on his promises of economic reform and pro-labor policies, strengthening organized unions and increasing workers' rights through social and industrial reforms.

Batista also maintained Cuba's alliance with the United States and, in 1941, when Pearl Harbor was attacked by the Japanese, he reacted swiftly by immediately declaring war on Japan in

A Cuban mob wrecks the government newspaper on July 13, 1933—the same day President Gerardo Machado was ousted from office.

support of President Franklin Roosevelt. Just days later, Cuba also declared war on Germany and Italy, the major fascist nations of World War II. During a visit to Washington, DC, in 1942, Batista also threw his diplomatic weight behind the United Nations' decision against the Spanish by denouncing the Spanish dictator Francisco Franco and declaring war on Spain.

The early part of the war in Europe had been characterized by tactical errors made by the former Cuban President Brú. These included his decision to turn away Jewish refugees aboard a German oceanliner, the MS St. Louis, who were thus sent back to Europe and ultimately killed in Nazi concentration camps. This misstep proved influential in Brú's 1940 election loss to Batista.

Unable to run for an additional presidential term at the conclusion of World War II, Batista appointed Carlos Zayas to be his successor. The plan failed when Ramón Grau fought a pro-union and labor campaign that secured him victory. With economic support from the United States as a direct consequence of Cuba's war endeavors, Grau presided over an economic boom, thanks in part to a price surge in sugar and a huge increase in global sugar demand. Grau also invested heavily in economic reforms, focusing on school building, social security benefits, and agricultural renewal.

Alongside the booming economy and infrastructure changes, Grau's presidency earned Cuba an international reputation for corruption and organized crime. The historic meeting of American Mafia and Cosa Nostra leaders took place in Havana in 1946. It was the first conference of its kind since the mobsters met in Atlantic City in 1929, and the repercussions of their decisions in Havana were felt across North America for decades.

Grau was succeeded as president by Carlos Prío Socarrás, who became even further embroiled in corruption and violence. In the next, the 1952 election, it seemed that the liberal-thinking Orthodox Party would be victorious. Eduardo Chibás led the liberal, democratic party on a platform of anticorruption and reform. Batista was struggling to find public support for his campaign when, shockingly, Chibás committed suicide fewer than 90 days before the poll.

Seizing this opportunity, Fulgencio Batista staged a bloodless coup to grab the presidency for himself, ousting Carlos Prío Socarrás. Batista immediately canceled the planned election and suspended the 1940 Constitution that he had played such a lead role in establishing. These undemocratic acts, when the election was finally held in 1953, Batista easily won and returned to the presidency.

The economic boom that Cuba enjoyed during the 1950s was largely guided by Batista's expansionist economic reforms. By 1958, Cuba's wages ranked among the top 10 nations globally, with its agricultural wages outstripping Germany, France, Denmark, and Belgium. Aided by an expanding middle class, Cuba's GDP rose higher than that of Japan and was on par with Italy. Labor reforms continued, and Cuban workers enjoyed many benefits denied to other nations even today. Paid vacation, sick leave, and maternity leave were all requirements, defying global norms.

Luxury and consumer goods also became readily available, with cars, telephones, and radios becoming commonplace and television ownership being the fifth highest in the world. Media expanded with hundreds of radio stations and dozens of daily newspapers. Cuba even boasted more cinemas than the far more densely populated New York City. Batista's health-care reforms were equally astonishing. The World Health Organization reported that Cuba's infant mortality rate was one of the lowest in the world and that it had a higher ratio of doctors per capita than almost any other nation. Education spending also increased, with adult literacy rates above 80 percent. It was a golden age for Cuba indeed.

However, the labor reforms came with a price. Large income disparities began to emerge between the highly regulated union workers and those languishing in the private sector. Restrictive practices by unions, particularly in regard to mechanization, condemned unemployed Cubans to a life of peasantry. The far larger American economy seemed more attractive for those not part of the labor movement, and the middle classes became fascinated by American media and culture.

Batista's labor regulations eventually led to economic stagnation. In addition, the economic regulations imposed during the 1950s began to have a stifling effect. Overseas and domestic investment declined considerably, and unemployment rates skyrocketed. The highly educated youth were unable to find work, as unions controlled almost all employment opportunities. Cuba's GDP fell, and by 1958, the growth rate was barely 1 percent annually.

During this period of declining economic fortune, Batista began to align himself with organized crime. Cuba was seen as a playground for the elite and Batista wanted to personally profit from the illegal activities. He soon developed close relationships with mob leaders Lucky Luciano and Meyer Lansky, and he created the "Latin Las Vegas," handing control of Havana's racetracks and casinos to Lansky and his mafia cohorts. Although officially banished to Sicily, Luciano secretly took up residence in Cuba.

Relaxed gambling laws and huge financial incentives for the construction of casinos, nightclubs, and hotels—all with tax kickbacks, fast-tracked licenses, and waived import duties—fueled the boom in gambling. Estimates were that Batista earned a daily income of 10 percent of the profits from various mob-run enterprises, with 30 percent going directly from Lansky's establishments to his Swiss bank accounts.

While the Mafia controlled both the legal and illegal entertainment on the island, almost all industry and commerce had come under the ownership of the United States. Private American companies owned most—if not all—of the Cuban sugar farms, mines, utilities, and oil industry. Resentment began to build as Americans generated profits from Cuban natural resources and labor. Batista himself cooperated with American interests and was rewarded with a gold-plated telephone when he approved huge increases in telephone rates by US-owned ITT. Batista also used the American aid programs to build up his arsenal of weaponry.

By 1953, Batista's indifference to the growing economic disparitites among Cubans fueled the aspirations of Marxist revolutionaries led by Fidel Castro. The Cuban Revolution began shortly after Batista's election. Although neither side seemed capable of halting the other, each won significant battles and delayed assigning a clear victor. But Castro was helped by the U.S. government, which encouraged Batista to flee Cuba. On January 1, 1959, Castro assumed control of Cuba.

Failing to find refuge in either the United States or Mexico, Batista eventually settled in Portugal, where he arrived with a personal fortune of more than $300 million and fine art valued at $700 million. Batista promised Portugal's leader, António Salazar, he would abstain from all political activity in return for protection. Batista became involved with insurance and real estate before dying of a heart attack in 1973, allegedly just before Castro implemented an assassination plan.

DID YOU KNOW

When Fulgencio Batista registered as a candidate in the 1940 election, he was rejected as no such name existed in courthouse records. Rumors circulated at the time, suggesting that a large bribe was paid to a judge to verify Batista's chosen name.

CUBAN MUSIC

FROM CELIA CRUZ TO PITBULL

RITA MONTANER

1920s & 1930s

Septepto Nacional
Trio Matamoros
Sexteto Boloña
Antonio Machín
The Lecuona
Cuban Boys

1960s & 1970s

1940s & 1950s

DESI ARNAZ

BENNY MORÉ

RAY BARRETTO

ARSENIO RODRÍGUEZ

CELIA CRUZ

LOS IRAKERE

SILVIO RODRÍGUEZ

The New Millennium

Osmani García
Eddy K
Gente de Zona

NOPE

1980s & 1990s

GLORIA ESTEFAN

BUENA VISTA SOCIAL CLUB

YES!

PITBULL

THE REVOLUTION
A QUICK STUDY

On July 26, 1953 Fidel Castro commanded about 160 revolutionaries to launch an attack on the Moncada Barracks in Santiago de Cuba. The date of the attack gave the the revolutionaries the name the 26th of July Movement.

The Castro brothers returned to Cuba from Mexico in the company of Guevara, Camilo Cienfuegos, and at least 80 insurgent guerrillas. Sailing aboard the cruiser Granma, the crew landed at Oriente Province on December 2, 1956.

By January 1957 rebels had overtaken an army outpost on the south coast and bolstered their ranks with volunteers, including many students.

Further success for the rebels came in May, when the army base of El Uvero fell. But soon after, one of their leaders, Frank País, was killed by police while protesting the Batista regime in Santiago de Cuba.

In February 1958 Raúl Castro led an insurrection that opened the Oriente's north coast to the rebel forces. Concerned that the Cuban government was losing ground, the US government suspended shipments of arms.

On April 9, 1958, following calls to all Cubans for a general revolt, a subsequent strike was only partially successful. Sensing a weakening in the rebels' resolve, Batista sent

10,000 troops to annihilate Castro's 300 armed guerrillas, but by August, the government militias were defeated.

In the first of many Cuban-US aircraft hijackings, an aircraft carrying weapons from Miami to Havana was captured, but it crashed.

Che Guevara led a successful attack on Santa Clara, seizing the capital of the Villa Clara province. Days later, Camilo Cienfuegos led the revolutionary guerrillas to victory in Yaguajay, effectively ending the revolution.

After seeking advice from the American government, Colonel Batista and his family fled Cuba on January 1, 1959, effectively handing over control of the country to Fidel Castro.

CHE GUEVARA
HERO OR FASCIST?

THE COMPLICATED LEGACY
OF CUBA'S ADOPTED LEADER

Perhaps an unlikely participant in the Cuban revolution, Ernesto "Che" Guevara was an Argentine Marxist revolutionary, who initially trained as a physician. From his very early life, Guevara was angered by the poverty he saw in his birthplace of Rosario. His father remarked that his partial Irish ancestry gave his eldest child his penchant for rebellion.

Though he suffered from bouts of asthma, Guevara strove to become a fine athlete as well as a master chess player. And surrounded by books in his parents' home, he became an avid reader, developing an interest in poetry. It was this interest that led Guevara tod the works of Karl Marx.

In 1948, Guevara began studying medicine at the University of Buenos Aires, but he often broke from his studies to take on lengthy expeditions satisfying his desire to explore. His first 2,800-mile journey on a motorized bicycle, in 1950, took him through much of northern Argentina. His second motor-cycle journey, lasting nine months and covering 5,000 miles, took him through almost all of South America.

During his introspective journeys, his radicalization formed as he was exposed to disease, hunger, and poverty.

It was during his intro-spective journeys that his radicalization formed, because he was exposed to disease, hunger, and poverty as he trav-eled extensively throughout South America. Guevara soon realized his most passionate belief: capitalist exploitation of Latin America by the United States needed to end. His first overt political involvement was in Guatemala, where he assisted President Jacobo Árbenz with extensive social reforms.

In September 1954, after marrying Hilda Gadea, Guevara moved to Mexico City, where he worked at a general hospital and lectured on medicine at the University of Mexico. In his spare time, he continued to document the poverty that surrounded him, recording the plight of the poor through photography for the Prensa Latina News Agency. Briefly, the Guevaras considered moving to Africa to extend his medical experience and treat people with the poorest health conditions. However, a meeting with Ñico López, an old friend who had been exiled from Cuba, changed these plans. Shortly thereafter, López introduced Guevara to Raúl Castro and, subsequently, to Raúl's brother Fidel.

Guevara was energized by his meetings with the Castro brothers and shared their view that US-controlled corporations and conglomerates were interfering with Cuban development while supporting oppressive regimes across all continents. Their anti-imperialist sensibilities forged a strong bond between them and, although it was his intention to be the 26th of July Movement's medic, Guevara took part in full military training with 80 other strong rebels under the guidance of General Alberto Bayo. Despite health issues and the arduous maneuvers practiced by the trainee rebels, by the completion of his training, Guevara was considered the strongest of the guerrillas.

ON COURSE WITH CASTRO

On November 25, 1956, a small band of trained guerillas, including Guevara, sailed with the Castro brothers on from Mexico to Cuba. They immediately began armed conflict with Batista's troops when they disembarked, and their numbers were reduced significantly. The government militia seemed to have the upper hand. Guevara discarded his medical supplies and grabbed ammunition. The change served to further fuel his passion for revolution.

Led by Frank País, the local rebels, known as campesinos, soon joined the survivors of the guerrillas task force as they retreated deep into the Sierra Maestra Mountains. Global speculation mounted that all the rebels had been wiped out, leading to an infamous *New York Times* article by Herbert Matthews ("Cuban Rebel is Visited in Hideout") that did much to create a lasting image of Fidel and the rebels as mythical legends. Guevara suffered heavily during this period of respite in the Sierra Maestra. He was allergic to mosquito bites and found himself covered in cysts. Still, being hidden among the poor farmers only served to harden Guevara's resolve. His anger at the absence of education, schooling, electricity, health care, and all other basic social provisions enjoyed by the city-based Cuban elite motivated him. He mobilized his skills to create schools and clinics, while, he began manufacturing grenades through makeshift factories and helped train new recruits. At this time he was appointed by Castro as the commander of a second army.

The elevation of his position to a formal rank as a guerrilla leader exposed a harsher side to Che's character, and his insistence on discipline began to manifest in frightening ways. He was known to shoot defectors, and deserters were treated as traitors. He even formed units to track down guerrillas who tried to leave the rebel unit. One such traitor was Eutimio Guerra, who admitted he had given information to Batista's troops, leading to the burning of many homes and villages. In his diary, Guevara follows his statement that he shot Guerra in the head at point-blank range with a vivid description of the wounds created by the bullet. Further evidence of his detachment came evident when he later published a memoir of the incident, *Death of a Traitor*.

Although the troops under his direction viewed Guevara as demanding and harsh, there was no question that he commanded enormous respect. One of the campesinos in his platoon, Tomás Alba, admitted that he would willingly lay down

Ernesto "Che" Guevara speaks with Fidel Castro as they review a peasant militia parade at the San Julian Base in Cuba.

his life for his commander. As part of his discipline, Che also saw his role as that of a teacher, and often made time for reading to entertain and educate his followers. This lent him what Castro described as a great moral authority over his troops.

As battles were joined and the rebel forces began to succeed with their incursions, Batista lost the support of arms supply from the United States. In July 1958, Guevara led his men against some 1,500 of Batista's forces, defeating their plans to encircle all of the rebel armies. Che's use of expert hit-and-run tactics succeeded in overcoming the larger force.

Dispatched on foot to secure Havana, Guevara led his men through night marches across the island, aiming to cut the island in half by seizing Las Villas Province during December 1958. In a series of brilliant tactical victories, his troops overtook

PAPA ERNEST

Few can rival the fascination that Che holds, but there was one man. Ernest "Papa" Hemingway lived in Cuba for many years. He penned some of his most famous works there, including The Old Man and the Sea *and* A Moveable Feast.

the province, except for the capital, Santa Clara. In his next mission with his squad, which was seen as the decisive battle of the entire revolution, he secured the capital. On December 31, 1958, Santa Clara fell to Guevara's forces, although confusion surrounded the exact nature of the conquest; due to some radio reports stating that Guevara had been killed. On January 1, 1959, hours after Batista had fled for the Dominican Republic, and six days before Fidel Castro, Guevara entered Havana and ended the Cuban revolution.

REVOLUTIONARY TO REFORMER

Now a conquering hero of the revolutionaries, Guevara's roles in the subsequent Castro-led regime began to shift public opinion away from his heroic status. Immediately after Castro seized power, Guevara retreated to Tarará to rest and recuperate from a violent asthma attack. There he ended his marriage to Hilda Gadea and made plans to marry his new partner, Aleida March.

When sufficiently recovered, Guevara was named commander of La Cabaña Fortress prison and was assigned to exact justice against the Batista supporters and armies. Guevara is said to have approved around 100 executions as punishment for those convicted by tribunals carried out at the prison. Some witnesses claim he almost relished the rituals of the firing squad. Humanitarian arguments did not seem to faze the newly hardened Guevara, and he saw his role as executioner as the only way to defend the revolution.

Guevara also focused on land reform. The Agrarian Reform Law he authored was implemented in May 1959, forbidding any foreignownership of Cuban sugar farms and redistributing land ownership to include peasants. Guevara's next role was as an international ambassador touring Asia, Africa, and Europe, where he met the leaders of seemingly allied nations. Castro was becoming concerned by Guevara's Marxist dogma and sent him abroad to distance himself. This also gave Castro time to gather more political power domestically—something Guevara was well aware of when he returned in September.

In response to international threats and attempts from right-wing nations to overturn Castro's regime, Castro appointed Guevara as minister of industry to speed up land reform. Guevara created the National Institute of Agrarian Reform, a force of some 100,000 militia who carried out vast land confiscations from American interests. In addition, he turned his attention to literacy projects, using close to 100,000 volunteers to form literacy brigades. This proved to be stunningly successful, bringing the literacy rate of the population up to about 96 percent, one of the highest literacy rates in the world. Guevara also expanded university education and ensured it was no longer accessible to only the white elite.

By 1961, not only was Guevera the minister of industry and made the de facto minister of education, but he was also appointed finance minister and president of the national bank. With virtual control of the Cuban economy, Guevara further implemented his Marxist ideology by instigating social reform to destroy any inequality in gender, race, or occupation. His goal was to create individual consciousness, scorning the tenets of socialism as insufficient for creating the new society Guevara favored. Volunteerism became a focus of his vision, and leading by example, he cut cane and worked in construction during his official time away from his ministries. Guevara also abolished all pay increases, instead awarding certificates of commendation for workers who exceeded their quotas; however, he also cut the pay of those who fell short.

INTERNATIONAL TIES

With less and less investment from the United States and Western Europe, Guevara visited many Eastern Bloc countries in Europe and began to court financial investors from Soviet-controlled economies. As the United States and the Soviet Union were engaged in the Cold War (1947-1991), according to Douglas Kellner, in anticipation of invasion, Guevara urged all Cuban people "… to learn to handle and … use firearms in defense of the nation." When news of Cuba's relationships spread, CIA-trained and sponsored, Brigade 2506, launched from Guatemala with the intention of overthrowing Castro and Communist Cuba. Brigade 2506 was defeated by Cuban armed forces within three days. Newspapers reporting details of the invasion attributed US forces' defeat to Guevara and Cuba's ties to the Soviet Union. It was believed that the CIA knew that Soviet forces had warned the Cuban government of a looming attack, but did not warn

Kennedy (who had approved Brigade 2506's mission) prior to invasion.

After Bay of Pigs, Guevara's stature on the world stage increased. He addressed the United Nations in December 1964, appearing on the American television show Face The Nation during his visit to New York. After an impassioned speech in Algeria, denouncing US and Soviet dominance of the Northern Hemisphere as being purposely calculated in order to destroy the Southern Hemisphere, Guevara disappeared.

Reappearing in Congo in early 1965, Guevara returned to his military rebel roots. He participated in other African wars before again disappearing, only to reemerge in Bolivia. In both Congo and Bolivia, Guevara's inability to develop relationships with the local rebel leaders resulted in his rejection from the very organizations he had come to support. Captured by CIA-backed forces of the Bolivian government, Guevara was executed by firing squad on October 9, 1967, on order of Bolivian President René Barrientos, despite American requests for him to be brought to Panama.

The romantic image of Guevara as a compassionate freedom fighter that educated, treated, and supported the illiterate peasants of Cuba grew. His image became a symbol for freedom across the world, and his life has been mythologized in theatrical and fictional works. The graphic image of Guevara's face—created by Irish artist Jim Fitzpatrick in 1968—continues to adorn merchandise across the globe as a symbol of youthful independence. The contradictions of his varying ethos remains, with many exiled Cubans viewing him as a butcher and a hated figure. But in Cuba itself, he remains a national hero, and his image adorns the three-peso banknote.

CHE ON SCREEN

CHE!

One of the first and most negatively received
films to dramatize the life of the Argentine guerilla fighter.

Year 1969
Playing Che Guevara Omar Sharif
Also starring Jack Palance, Robert Loggia
Trivia Critic Harry Medved included the movie in his book
The Fifty Worst Films of All Time.

EVITA

Che narrates the story of Eva Perón. There is some doubt if this is
Che Guevara at all. Certainly Perón and Guevara were not known
to have any genuine connection in life.

Year 1996
Playing Che Guevara Antonio Banderas
Also starring Madonna and Jonathan Pryce
Trivia The film earned an Oscar for best original song.

FIDEL

A miniseries developed for television that is almost a documentary in the way facts are dramatized.

Year 2002

Playing Che Guevara Gael García Bernal

Also starring Victor Huggo Martin and Maurice Compte

Trivia When adapted for home video release, the film was cut by almost 50 minutes.

THE MOTORCYCLE DIARIES

A Spanish film that dramatizes young Che's 1952 travels across South America.

Year 2004

Playing Che Guevara Gael García Bernal

Also starring Rodrigo de la Serna

Trivia Awarded the British Academy Award for the best film not in the English language.

CHE

A two-part biopic divided into *Che Part 1: The Argentine* and *Che Part 2: Guerrilla*.

Year 2008

Playing Che Guevara Benicio del Toro

Also starring Demián Bichir and Rodrigo Santoro

Trivia Del Toro won the best actor prize at the Cannes Film Festival.

CUBA UNDER CASTRO(S)

REVOLUTIONARY FORCES TAKE HOLD OF THE ISLAND

After installing himself as prime minister, Fidel Castro's initial period of government leadership was unsettled. Anti-revolutionary feelings in Cuba were strong, and many feared the Marxist doctrine and socialist policies being pursued. In addition, the U.S. government, which, after abandoning Batista as the revolution had reached its conclusion, now opposed Castro's new regime.

On first hearing reports of the presence of Soviet missiles in Cuba, the Kennedy White House dismissed Republican concerns, writing them off as electioneering.

Castro acted swiftly to eliminate opposing voices from the Cuban government and citizens, turning against many organizations that had once supported revolution. All media was brought under state control, and any newspapers voicing dissent were shut down. Even labor unions that appeared to oppose any of the intended new policies were declared illegal and disbanded.

Despite Castro's attempts to stifle opposition and take control of all aspects of government, many counter-revolutionary groups sprang up, shielding themselves by forming battalions in the mountainous regions of the island. Led by Rafael Trujillo, with help from the CIA and the Dominican Republic's government, attacks were regularly carried out on Castro-controlled military bases and government buildings. This period became known as the Escambray Rebellion, which some estimates suggest involved more troops than the Cuban Revolution itself. The Escambray Rebellion lasted until 1965, when the government troops finally defeated the rebels.

Politically, Castro made moves to create a single-party state as early as 1961 by bringing together the nation's political parties under the Integrated Revolutionary Organizations, later known as the United Party of the Cuban Socialist Revolution in March 1962. By 1965, it was officially known as the Communist Party, with Castro as first secretary. Although other parties were allowed to exist, the subsequent rewriting of Cuba's constitution, which was ratified by almost 98 percent of the population in 1976, mandated that political parties were not permitted to challenge Castro in election.

The United States officially recognized the new regime on January 7, 1961. However, President Eisenhower and the American government showed much concern about the new political

Che Guevara and Fidel Castro in Cuba, 1961.

landscape. Eisenhower initially expected Cuba to remain an ally of the United States. Even those who were fundamentally opposed to the Batista regime expected the relationship with the United States to continue along similar lines.

A continuation of US-Cuban relations was impossible, and within six months of Castro seizing power, the US government began making plans to remove him from office. Eisenhower pressured allied nations to cease all weapon and war machinery sales to Cuba, and the CIA began arming independent guerrilla blocs, or territories, within Cuba. Although no publicly declared pressure was placed on the French government to cease arms trades, the CIA was blamed when the French vessel La Coubre was destroyed by an explosion in Havana as it unloaded military equipment and munitions.

Further pressure was placed on international oil companies Texaco, Esso (Standard Oil), and Royal Dutch Shell to reject attempts to refine Soviet crude oil in the Cuban refineries once they came under state control in 1960. Each move by the United States to block Cuban progress was met by a response along the same vein from Castro's government. For instance, Castro nationalized the Cuban oil industry and seized control of US-owned businesses and properties including the United Fruit

Company and ITT. All land owned by foreigners was also seized and redistributed.

SPLITTING WITH THE STATES

On January 3, 1961, following the annual New Year's Day parade, (held in Havana and displaying Soviet weaponry, tanks, and missiles), the United States severed all diplomatic ties with Cuba and withdrew its ambassador, Philip Bonsal. This action laid ground for a plan devised under the Eisenhower administration but executed during the leadership of new US President John F. Kennedy. Fearing the buildup of vast military equipment and supplies from the Soviets, the military launched the Bay of Pigs invasion—a failed, disastrous incursion that crushed the young president's reputation.

The CIA sponsored the invasion (which included in its troops 1,400 Cuban exiles), but Kennedy accepted responsibility for its ultimate failure. Receiving international press coverage, the invasion had the unwanted effect of strengthening international support for Cuba. Defeated but not deterred, the US continued with plans to overthrow Castro by stealthy means, including the covert Operation Mongoose. So began the arming of counter-revolutionary guerrillas and sabotaging Cuba's infrastructure.

Over the next year, the Kennedy administration implemented many draconian policies to destabilize Cuba's regime. In February 1963, all US citizens were barred from making any commercial, financial, and travel transactions with Cuba. Kennedy was less successful when his administration lobbied other nations to implement embargoes; Cuba managed to continue trading with Asia and Europe.

Castro continued to fear US intervention, and his somewhat justified paranoia, led him to form alliances with other communist regimes for protection, most notably the Soviet Union. Secretly, Castro agreed to allow the Soviets to deploy a large number of medium-range nuclear missiles within Cuba. The Americans themselves had already deployed similar missiles covertly in both Italy and Turkey, to counter the stockpiles the Soviets had moved into Eastern Europe. In a secret meeting, Soviet leader Nikita Khrushchev agreed to place nuclear arms within Cuba as a defense against American intervention. Cuban dissenters became aware of the Soviet weaponry buildup and alerted their exiled comrades.

The US Air Force began flying over Cuba, photographing areas of concern, which soon exposed the Soviet missile activity. Kennedy's administration immediately established a naval quarantine around Cuba's waters, designed to stop any further Soviet ships arriving on the island. Tense negotiations began between the US president and Soviet leader Khrushchev through the United Nations. Partly in fear of the US naval force being sent to the area, but also in response to Castro's extremism, the 13-day standoff that brought the world to the brink of nuclear war played out across the globe's TV screens. It ended when the Soviets turned their ships around.

The Americans were forced to agree never to invade Cuba in return for the Soviets removing all their bases on the island, and on November 20, 1962, the Cuban Missile Crisis officially ended. One unforeseen effect the crisis had for Castro's Cuba was that relations between Moscow and Washington were strengthened.

THE RICH DITCH

The establishment of the socialist political system (as it was still described) resulted in the wholesale exodus of the wealthy upper and middle classes. The drain of commercial and business expertise had dire effects on the economic well-being of the island. Some groups, notably those of Jewish faith, were permitted to relocate to Israel, and those who had ancestral links to Spain were also able to relocate, to the Iberian Peninsula. Many more attempted to leave, leading to a formal agreement with the United States in 1965 to airlift Cubans into the country. Over the next five years, some 250,000 Cubans took advantage of the agreement and settled in the United States. Many others fled to Spain, Italy, Canada, and Mexico. Just as many others escaped unofficially by boat.

Cuba's isolation from the United States did not deter Castro's government from pressing ahead with social and economic reforms. By 1965, forced labor units were established, and thousands of counter-revolutionaries and dissenters were sent to these concentration camps. Dissent continued nonetheless, and by the early 1970s the standard of living in Cuba had fallen dramatically. As many as 20,000

DID YOU KNOW

Post-revolution, Fidel's brother Raúl Castro was appointed to command the Revolutionary Armed Forces. He introduced a local defense system known as Committees for the Defense of the Revolution, which was composed of citizens prepared to be government informants on their neighborhood activity.

dissidents a year were reportedly captured, tortured, and isolated in the camps, where conditions were inhumane. Many were simply executed, and some 33,000 people are thought to have been killed during the first decade of Castro rule. Unemployment began to rise, but to counter this, the Cuban government simply made unemployment illegal under a 1971 labor law that jailed anyone without work, offering them military service in Soviet wars within Africa as an alternative to concentration camps.

AN ECONOMY IN FREEFALL

With little foreign trade and few exports, no upper class and a spartan middle class, entanglement in foreign conflicts, and a population decline, Cuba's economy stuttered to the brink of collapse during the 1970s and 1980s. By 1989, Cuba's economic crisis was so severe that the Special Period in Time of Peace was declared. This period of economic depression was largely fueled by the collapse of the Soviet Union in the early 1990s. Severe shortages of gasoline and diesel oil meant automobiles and mechanized factories became unsustainable. Life in Cuba was again transformed.

The Soviet Union had been Cuba's biggest trading ally, accounting for 80 percent of all exports and imports. Soviet oil was vital to Cuba's economy, not only to satisfy its own consumption needs, but also as an export commodity when excess petroleum was sold internationally for large profits. With the supply discontinued, Cuba's GDP fell 34 percent, and food and medical imports stopped almost completely. Agriculture was hit badly, too, as all the farm machinery used to cultivate crops became useless without the fuel to run them.

Millions of jobs were lost in factories and in the highly mechanized farming areas. Since Cuba was no longer able to supply the Soviets with their vast sugar manufacture (in exchange for oil), it needed to establish new crops. Fruit and vegetable farming was initiated, which had a positive impact on the eating habits of the Cuban people whose diet previously consisted of lots of meat and dairy. Unfortunately, there still simply wasn't enough food to go around.

Cubans resorted to any method available to put meat on their tables.

Power outages, a collapse in public transport, and food shortages became the norm. Castro's government responded with encouragement for organic farming. With help from scientists and farmers from Australia, new farming techniques were taught to offset hunger and malnutrition. Throughout this period, US humanitarian aid, in addition to Venezuelan support, became more necessary, especially after the election of the socialist Hugo Chavez in 1998.

Famine spread widely, and Cubans resorted to any method available to put meat on their tables. Such was the scarcity of cows and sheep, that it was made illegal to kill any farm animal. Cubans began to eat cats, dogs, and, reportedly, many of the animals kept within zoos simply disappeared.

With food distribution in the hands of the government, the military and elite classes were given priority in food allocation.

The famines created epidemics of disease and illness, with huge numbers of deaths from diabetes, stroke, neuropathy, and heart disease. By 1993, the average calorie intake per day for Cubans had fallen to around 1,450 per person, far lower than the recommended 2,000. In addition, overcrowding became commonplace as building programs collapsed. In turn, urban areas became excessively overcrowded as rural communities failed. The Cuban government introduced a program of land distribution to encourage rural living, which implemented crop exchanges and cooperative farming.

ANOTHER REVOLUTION?

August 1994 saw the first signs of mass public dissent. Thousands took to the streets to protest, chanting for freedom and hurling rocks and missiles at the police.

Seeing an opportunity to exploit the growing unrest gripping the nation, and hoping to destabilize Castro further, the Clinton administration took steps to tighten laws concerning Cuba. In March 1996, the Helms-Burton Act was signed into law. The act imposed penalties on any international company doing business with Cuba, making any kind of foreign trade virtually impossible if those same companies were doing business with the United States.

Although the August 1994 demonstration had been dispersed fairly effortlessly, dissident groups began to grow in strength. *La Patria es de Todos* (The Homeland Belongs to All) was a petition signed by thousands of Cubans and delivered to members of Parliament, who were forced to give it consideration despite dismissing it on technical grounds. When former US President

Jimmy Carter visited Cuba in 2002, he vocally championed the petition, which called for a referendum on the political process governing the island nation. To silence the dissenting voices, Castro issued a proclamation that his interpretation of socialist ideology would be the law of the land.

The Helms-Burton Act and the support shown internationally to dissident groups continued to hurt the Cuban economy and began to affect Castro's regime as well as his health. By 2006, his health had deteriorated to such a degree that he announced he was withdrawing from public life. A year later, he named his brother Raúl as acting president. On February 18, 2008, Castro formally renounced the presidency and affirmed he would never seek political office again.

FIDEL'S FAR REACH

CUBA'S MILITARY IN AFRICA

One of Cuba's revolutionary socialist ambitions was to expand its influence abroad and gain new foreign allies through international actions. At first, these overseas adventures mainly focused on health and education. Later, they also covered military training and development. These were key factors that disturbed US leadership and, to a lesser degree, the Soviet Union, Cuba's main global ally.

GUANTÁNAMO A SHORT HISTORY

1898

JUNE The first US troops land on Cuba during the Spanish-American War, establishing a camp at Guantánamo Bay.

1903

FEBRUARY In exchange for approx. $4,085 today, President Teddy Roosevelt leases Guantánamo Bay, almost 46 sq. miles of territory.

1934

FEBRUARY President Franklin D. Roosevelt visits Guantánamo Bay aboard the USS Houston.

JUNE The lease is revised: the land will revert to Cuban control if abandoned or agreed by both governments.

1939

Cuba was highly involved in many African conflicts, supporting left-wing governments and liberation movements across the continent. Most notably, Cuba's military support for the Marxist People's Movement for the Liberation of Angola (MPLA) enabled the MPLA to wage its fight during the protracted Angolan Civil War (1975-2002).

Civil war began in Angola shortly after the country's liberation from Portugal. The lengthy civil war was one of the many bloody battlefields on which broader Cold War politics played out. The two sides in the unrest were the MPLA and the National Union for the Total Independence of Angola militia (UNITA). Although they had initially shared a socialist political ideology and had fought together in the war for independence, the two factions went head to head in the civil war. The MPLA claimed a Marxist-Leninist agenda, and was supported by the Soviet Union and Cuba. UNITA, backed by South Africa and the United States, adopted an anti-communist ideology.

1940 APRIL Naval Base is established and begins operating.

JULY Construction begins to expand the facilities at Guantanamo.

1941

FEBRUARY President Harry Truman visits the base.

1948 JANUARY The Cuban Revolution ends with the establishment of the Castro-led socialist state. All US military are withdrawn.

1959

Cuba had supported the MPLA (which identified its struggle to be free from Portuguese colonization as similar to Cuba's own overthrow of Spanish rule) from the beginning of the war for independence in 1961.

Cuba's military attention was also drawn to North Africa, where Castro's government openly supported the Algerian National Liberation Front against its French colonial rulers. Almost as soon as Algeria gained independence in 1962, a border dispute with Morocco flared up and Cuba immediately dispatched troops to fight alongside Algerian forces.

Shortly after securing victory for Algeria, Cuba offered support to the Simba Rebellion in Congo. The quasi-communist Simba had rebelled against the Congolese government in 1964, but it suffered heavy defeats and casualties. Both the USSR and Cuba sent troops and equipment, with military advisers led by Che Guevara joining the Simba rebels. Under Guevara's direction and Soviet guidance, the rebels became a far more efficient military force but still

GUANTÁNAMO A SHORT HISTORY

1961

OCTOBER Guantánamo Bay is evacuated as troops arrive to protect the base during the Cuban Missile Crisis.

JANUARY Diplomatic links between Cuba and the USA are severed. President Eisenhower declares this does not impact Guantánamo Bay.

1962

SEPTEMBER To accommodate almost 34,000 Haitian refugees, temporary housing is constructed at the base.

1991

OCTOBER Further expansion of the refugee shelters is developed to accommodate 11,000 Cubans claiming asylum.

1994

struggled against the more efficient troops of the African National Congress (ANC), which supported the Congolese armies. By the time the rebellion failed, Guevara was suffering from dysentery and was highly disillusioned by the entire enterprise.

With the end of Portugal's colonization of Angola, both the MPLA and UNITA took control of various regions within the country. The MPLA violently forced out the National Liberation Front of Angola (FNLA). This succeeded in alarming other African nations, such as South Africa and Zaire, which both sent troops and military equipment into the country to bolster UNITA troops. In response to this, and without consulting with the USSR, Cuba organized Operation Carlota sending 18,000 troops to support the MPLA, which proved decisive in defeating South African troops and preventing UNITA from advancing further into MPLA territory.

South African leader John Vorster secretly agreed to keep Cuban troops within Angola and continue to use Cuban military support. However, when the plan was discovered by Soviet

1996 APRIL President Clinton draws up plans to accommodate Kosovan refugees at the naval base, but then abandons the plans.

2002 JANUARY President Obama orders that the detention center close within a year. Detainees are still held there in 2015.

MAY The refugee centers at Guantánamo Bay close. Most Cuban refugees are evacuated to the US and Haitians sent home.

1999

JANUARY Guantánamo Bay naval base opens as a detention center and accepts the first 20 prisoners from Afghanistan.

2009

intelligence, 60 Soviet officers were sent to lead more deployed Cuban troops. Under their directive, Cuba was forbidden from intervening in in the civil unrest. Instead, the Soviets said, Cuba's mission was to contain and repel South African troops.

During 1975 and 1976, most foreign forces withdrew from the conflict, except Cuba. In February 1976, rather than scaling back its military presence as both Portugal and South Africa concluded their involvement, Cuba had sent in an additional 6,000 troops to Angola, increasing its military presence to 11,000 soldiers.

Worried by the escalation of Cuba's involvement and that it was masterminded by Moscow, US President Gerald Ford authorized covert action through Operation IA Feature, designed to support UNITA and FNLA. Secretary of State Henry Kissinger was warned that the US involvement could not remain secret for long and that the USSR would escalate its involvement and support for Cuban troops in retaliation. Resignations from the State Department, in addition to Democratic party Senator Dick Clark's South African fact-finding mission to South Africa exposed Ford's plans, leading Congress to pass legislation forbidding any aid to private groups engaged in military or paramilitary operations in Angola.

In reality, neither the United States nor the USSR wanted to become involved in the Angolan conflict. The United States saw it as a potential "second Vietnam," and the Soviets were focused on winning the Cold War across Europe. Although the Soviet alliance with the MPLA continued, there was no escalation in military support.

Cuban troops helped the MPLA secure the entire southern region of Angola by 1977. By that time, Castro had also become embroiled in support of the Ethiopian Red Terror—a violent political campaign that spread across Ethiopia and Eritrea, spearheaded by the Marxist dictator Mengistu Haile Mariam. Several genocidal campaigns that killed thousands of people were credited to Mariam. He was convicted of all.

Castro maintained support for Mariam, even in his battle against the Somalian Marxist dictator Siad Barre. Shortly after the outbreak of the Ethio-Somali war in July 1977, Cuba sent 11,000 troops to support the Soviet-armed Ethiopian troops. The Cuban intervention proved decisive in driving out Barre's Somali forces.

By the early 1980s, Cuban troops in various parts of Africa had increased exponentially. Some 50,000 soldiers were stationed in Angola, where fighting continued through 1988, and 24,000 were stationed in Ethiopia after the Ogaden battles of the Ethio-Somali War were executed successfully. Additionally, Cuba provided strategic support in the Mozambican Civil War.

In December 1988, representatives from Cuba, Angola, and South Africa signed the Tripartite Accord, finally ending Cuba's involvement in the conflict that began in 1975. Cuba's support was seen as crucial in securing the MPLA's control over vast areas of the nation and securing Namibia's independence. The Tripartite Accord also signaled the end of all military engagement by Cuba in Africa, therefore ensuring the withdrawal of all Cuban soldiers from Congo and Ethiopia.

FROM THE CRADLE TO THE GRAVE

HEALTH AND SOCIAL SERVICES IN CASTRO'S CUBA

Even before the Cuban Revolution, Cuba was internationally renowned for its health and social benefits. Several Cuban doctors received global recognition for their work, particularly in the study of yellow fever. Life expectancy in Cuba was higher than almost any other nation in the region—especially as compared to the Caribbean—and more doctors, nurses, and hospitals were available per capita than many European nations. Still, health care was centralized in urban areas, so Cubans living in cities and larger towns were cared for significantly better than those in rural areas.

Immediately following the revolution, the new leaders pledged universal health care as a cornerstone of state planning. One of the key foundations for health-care reform was Che Guevara's speech, "On Revolutionary Medicine." Unfortunately, the embargo imposed by the US government derailed many of the planned social reforms, and disease and infant mortality rates began to rise. As early as 1960, the new government implemented a program of nationalization of all medical services. This led to numerous doctors, health workers, and medical students fleeing the island for the United States. Such a drain on available human resources adversely affected Cuban health. However, thanks to the implementation of universal, free-education programs, and the previously declining doctor-patient ratio began to grow steadily as more options for training was established.

Mass vaccination programs resulted in the eradication of a number of contagions, including polio and rubella. Although economic hardship increased cases of chicken pox and hepatitis. By 1970, a focus on prenatal care helped reduce the infant mortality rate.

In 1962, a program of food rationing was introduced as another key social reform. Basic food provisions were provided to all citizens, if accompanied by ration vouchers, at nominal cost. Government stores were introduced to dispense rations, which included rice, beans, potatoes, bread, and eggs, as well as small amounts of meat. In 2015, it is estimated that the provisions supplied

HELPING HANDS

Today, Cuba provides a higher level of medical personnel to the Third World than the entire G8 group—France, Germany, Italy, the UK, Japan, the United States, Canada, and Russia—combined.

by the state would cost the average American $50 to purchase, whereas Cubans pay around $1.20 for the same food.

The collapse of the Soviet Union and the subsequent loss of its long-standing subsidies negatively impacted many social welfare programs in Cuba, leading to famine. Food distribution collapsed and aid programs were slow to respond, largely due to Cuban reluctance to accept them. US aid was finally allowed in 1993.

Today, despite the ideal of free health care outlined in the constitution, a black market still flourishes. Doctors are prepared to expedite treatments and diagnoses—such as x-rays—for cash payments or gifts provided by patients in lieu of monetary rewards. Medicines that are not available within Cuba are often illegally imported by Cubans with relatives in the United States or elsewhere and then privately sold.

About 20,000 paying health "tourists" are treated in Cuba each year, adding at least $40 million to the economy. Although tourist hospitals are managed separately, this practice, which has built up over the last 20 years, has affected state health providers.

One of the driving ideals of Che Guevara's vision was to alleviate the third-world status of many nations, particularly those in Africa, by encouraging and, at some times forcing the sharing of international medical resources.

Guevara went to Africa to use his medical training and expertise to treat fighters, and also to educate the local population on medical matters.

Although Guevara's goal was certainly unsuccessful in his lifetime, the Cuban government recognized the importance of exporting its medical knowledge and expertise. By joining international organizations such as UNICEF and WHO, Cuba has become a key player in international advances in health care.

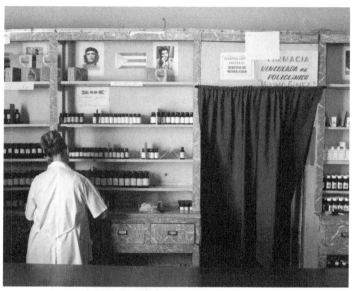

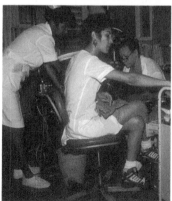

A pharamacy in Holguin, Cuba; a dentist's office in Las Tunas, Cuba; a mother
and her injured son after visiting the doctor, Cuba, 2011.

Cuba estimates that it has about 25,000 doctors deployed in various parts of the world, and its medical teams have served in several natural and humanitarian disaster relief operations. Additionally, Cuba has accepted nearly 20,000 children (from the areas affected by the Chernobyl nuclear power station) for treatment in Cuba for radiation sickness.

Other advantages of the Cuban economy for medical trade have been explored in Venezuela, where Cuba provides doctors and medical staff in exchange for oil. This has been a particularly successful endeavor and has dramatically helped the poorest Venezuelans with limited access to health care. Not all in the Venezuelan opposition parties welcomed this arrangement because many feared the doctors were working as "Fidel's ambassadors." Many Cuban doctors have risen rapidly to positions of power within Venezuela's medical services industry. Dissenters claim these roles are beyond Cuban training and, as a result, there are cases of Venezuelans refusing to be treated by Cuban medical staff.

Other critics of the export of Cuban doctors note that these doctors are still paid at Cuban wage levels abroad and that their families are forbidden to travel with them. Even under these circumstances, the Cuban American National Foundation, which examines human rights issues, has noted that many Cuban doctors have defected to the United States while working abroad.

Pharmaceutical research, development, and manufacture have recently become a very large part of the Cuban economy. As a result, many vaccines and medical products are exported globally. Because the same medicines are not provided or available to the local population, alternative health care has experienced growth, particularly in regard to herbal medicine, which is officially recognized by the Ministry of Health. Herbal medicine is so widely recognized that medicinal use of plants is included in the school curriculum.

THE TOP

10
FAMOUS CUBANS

1
Carlos Finlay (1833–1915) Juan Carlos Finlay y Barres was the internationally recognized pioneer in the field of research for yellow fever, credited as the first scientist to recognize that the transmission of the disease was through mosquitos.

2
Teófilo Stevenson (1952–2012) Stevenson is one of only three boxers to win three Olympic gold medals—the first in the sport in Cuban history. The BBC described Stevenson as "Cuba's greatest boxer, one of its most famous figures after Castro."

3
Alicia Alonso (1921–) Alicia Ernestina de la Caridad del Cobre Martínez Hoya (above) is a partially blind prima ballerina who founded the Ballet Nacional de Cuba in 1955. Alonso attracted world fame for her portrayals of Carmen and Giselle. She has won numerous international awards for her performances and choreography.

4 Eligio Sardiñas Montalvo (1910–1988)

Famous around the world as Kid Chocolate, Sardiñas was a Cuban boxer who became the first fighter from his nation to be declared world champion in the junior lightweight division at the age of 21. Through his career, Montalvo won 136 bouts and had only 10 losses.

5 Ana Fideli Quirot (1963–)

Ana Fidelia Quirot Moré is the two-time world champion athlete who competed at both 400- and 800-meter distance running. She won gold medals at the World Championships, World Cup, and Pan American Games during the 1980s and 1990s.

6 Alberto Díaz Gutiérrez (1928–2001)

Better known as Alberto Korda, or simply Korda (left), Gutiérrez was the official photographer for Fidel Castro and friends. Gutiérrez's image of Che Guevara, named "Guerrillero Heroico," produced in 1960, became a universal symbol of revolution and rebellion. (See image on page 42)

7
José Raúl Capablanca (1888–1942) José Raúl Capablanca y Graupera was the world chess champion from 1921 to 1927. His exceptional speed made him almost impervious to defeat. He lost only 35 games in his career, leading to his nickname, "the Human Chess Machine."

8
Desi Arnaz (1917–1986) Desiderio Alberto Arnaz y de Acha III (below) became famous for his marriage and TV partnership with American actress Lucille Ball, with whom he appeared on the globally syndicated *I Love Lucy* show. Arnaz was also a renowned musician through his Latin band, the Desi Arnaz Orchestra.

9
José Canseco (1964–) José Canseco Capas played major league baseball for Oakland Athletics and Texas Rangers, but his career ended when his tell-all autobiography revealed his performance-enhancing drug use and widespread steroid use in the sport.

10
Compay Segundo (1907–2003) Máximo Francisco Repilado Muñoz was a multi-instrumentalist who rose to international fame with his band's album *Buena Vista Social Club*, winning multiple Grammy Awards.

CUBAN CIGARS

Tobacco cultivation covers the entire island of Cuba. Leaves are mixed for manufacture from various plantations, a somewhat unusual practice in cigar production. Many cigar experts praise Cuba's cigar rollers, or *torcedores*, as the most highly skilled in the world. They are also held in high esteem within Cuban society. Although not as economically important as the sugar industry, Cuban cigars are undoubtedly the country's most famous export.

The growth of tobacco and the manufacture of cigars are government controlled through two state companies, Cubatabaco and Habanos SA.

After harvesting, the leaves are aged and dried using heat and water, a process that can take up to 45 days to complete.

The dried leaves are then sorted into either filler or wrapper. The highest-quality cigars are handmade by torcedores, although lesser-quality cigars can be entirely machine processed. Cuban leaves generally use different varieties of tobacco for the filler—a bound bunch of tobacco leaves folded by hand—and the wrapper, which is the the most expensive component, and it determines the cigar's character and flavor. Traditionally, a third element, called a binder, is added to separate the filler and outer wrapping layer.

While the wrapper will not be the sole source of a cigar's flavor, darker wrappers tend to produce a sweeter flavor, whereas lighter wrappers are generally thought to create a "dry" smoke and taste.

After rolling, the cigars are laid down for aging, a process that can take decades. As long as the temperature and humidity are maintained, there is no reason why a cigar would not stay in perfect condition for all that time.

Cuban cigars remain one of the island's leading and most important exports, with some 60 million cigars exported annually. Cuban cigars, previously held as a highly desired product in the United States, with widespread smuggling, can now be purchased by American citizens licensed to travel in Cuba (per Obama's actions to chart a new course with Cuba explained on page 102).

The loosening of the trade embargo in January 2015 and the easing of travel restrictions permits US citizens to legally import cigars from Cuba, as they are allowed to purchase up to $100 worth of tobacco and alcohol per visit for personal use.

AN ECONOMY OF EMBARGOES

STABILITY AND LIMITED TRADE

The challenging relationship between Cuba and the United States has been defined by a series of embargoes imposed at various times by the United States since the revolution that brought Fidel Castro to power. Each embargo has had varying effects on the Cuban economy, with some observers arguing that often the undesired effect of sanctions has been to strengthen Castro's position.

A march against the Bush Administration's measures to strengthen the blockade in Havana, Cuba.

Protesters in Miami fight for a break in the trade embargo against Cuba.

Although not specifically created to deal with Cuban relations, the 1917 "Trading with the Enemy Act" has been cited as the justification for many of the subsequent embargoes imposed by Congress since the revolution ended in 1959.

During the revolution, in 1958, President Eisenhower imposed an arms embargo, which did more to harm the US-supported Batista regime than it did the rebel forces. With the arms embargo still in place after the end of the revolution, the Soviet Union took over supplying arms to Cuba. The Americans retaliated by reducing their sugar imports from the island to just 700,000 tons, which, in turn, encouraged the USSR to buy the remaining sugar surplus.

In 1960, the first official trade embargo was imposed after Cuba seized the American-owned oil refineries and nationalized them, thus, permitting the refining of Soviet oil. This first embargo prohibited US businesses from selling goods to Cuba with the exception of food and medicine. Cuba nationalized all American businesses and properties to counter the measure, leading to Eisenhower cutting all diplomatic ties in January 1961.

In February 1962, President Kennedy signed an executive order forbidding all imports of any goods containing Cuban materials, and this was followed by orders to suspend aid to any nation that provided assistance to Cuba. Despite the full trade embargo in place, nonsubsidized food and medicine were exempted.

Travel restrictions were first imposed in 1963 at the height of the Cuban Missile Crisis. Additionally, under the Cuban Assets Control Regulations issued in July 1963, all Cuban assets within the United States were frozen.

Under Jimmy Carter's presidency, the travel embargo lapsed and regulations that had previously prohibited American dollars being spent in Cuba were eased. In 1982, President Ronald Reagan reinstated the trade embargo, making the dollar

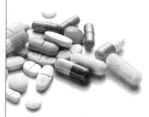

GOODS RELIEF

There was some easing of the Helms-Burton Act in 2000, when the sale of agricultural goods and medicine to Cuba was permitted based on humanitarian grounds.

unavailable to Cubans once more, but travel restrictions were not reimposed.

The Cuban Democracy Act in 1992 and the later, more stringent Helms-Burton Act in 1996 further strengthened sanctions. Despite objections from the European Union, these acts imposed penalties on foreign companies doing business of any kind in Cuba and, as a further consequence, those companies would be banned from doing business in the United States. Additionally, the leadership of any company engaged in commerce with Cuba would be banned from entering the United States.

The impact of the embargoes had mixed results and implications for political leadership although they all undoubtedly squeezed the Cuban economy. Establishing stronger ties with the Soviet Union helped alleviate some of the earlier restrictions. However, the collapse of the USSR in the early 1990s severely crippled Cuban economic prospects. Other trading nations were reluctant to antagonize the United States, even before the Helms-Burton Act officially banned them from doing so. For instance, British Petroleum was deterred from its keen interest of exploring offshore drilling projects with Cuba due to the effect on US relations. Royal Dutch Shell and Clyde Petroleum also abandoned plans to invest.

The Cuban government concedes that embargoes cost its economy about $700 million annually. The US Chamber of Commerce claims the loss in Cuban sales and exports to be a far higher figure of $1.2 billion. The Cuba Policy Foundation, a self-styled, nonpartisan think tank, similarly estimates that the US economy is losing $3.6 billion annually through lost economic opportunities because of the embargoes.

The United Nations has been a strong critic of the American embargoes and has had particularly scathing commentary about their negative effects on the Cuban population. Medical crises within Cuba often result from a basic lack of clean water and soap, leading to raised levels of infectious diseases. Canada and the EU remain outspoken critics of the Helms-Burton Act, claiming that it solidifies the regime's position within Cuba, as the people see the United States as the enemy state.

Following the December 2014 prisoner exchanges, both presidents Obama and Raúl Castro announced moves to ease restrictions and reestablish diplomatic relations. President Obama has since taken steps for Congress to review all existing embargoes and restrictions.

THE CUBAN DIASPORA

WHERE HAVE CUBANS GONE?

rior to the Ten Years' War (1868–1878), there were very few emigrants out of Cuba. Cuba was a prosperous society. But the war changed this dramatically, and Cubans sought political asylum within the United States and other countries to escape the conflicts. Migration rapidly accelerated following the 1959 revolution, and estimates are that more than a million Cubans have since settled in the United States, Spain, Mexico, Italy, and Canada, as well as many other nations.

Immediately following the revolution, many Cubans temporarily fled to the area around Miami. Expecting the new Castro government to be fairly short lived and to return once order had been reestablished. They left behind property, cars, and other assets with their friends, family, and neighbors, only to discover that Castro's regime moved quickly to seize them all. As a result, those who had moved to the United States were forced to claim refugee status with the American authorities.

As it became clear that Castro's regime was not going to be a "90-day-wonder," families began to fear for the safety of their children. The Catholic Church organized a scheme called Operation Peter Pan to help 14,000 children of various faiths relocate to foster care within the United States. The children evacuated were generally in their later teens, but many children as young as six years were included. Teenage boys made up the bulk of the numbers as their parents were anxious to avoid their conscription into the Cuban army.

The Bay of Pigs invasion increased immigration significantly in 1961, as it was clear the rebel government was

The population of Miami—pictured here—is 34 percent Cuban, which has significantly shaped the city's culture and nightlife.

there to stay. From 1965 to 1973, the respective administrations of Kennedy, Johnson, and Nixon operated programs that airlifted refugees twice daily to Miami. Close to 300,000 Cubans took advantage of these "Freedom Flights," as they became the only way to leave Cuba legally. Others took more drastic action, including a group that crashed a bus into Havana's Peruvian embassy to claim asylum.

The US Coast Guard was unable to cope with the sudden arrival of fishing boats, small boats, and large shrimping vessels, packed with Cubans.

Flotillas of refugees began leaving Cuba in higher density during the 1980s. Over 100,000 people escaped in such a short period of time that the US Coast Guard was unable to cope with the sudden arrival of fishing boats, small boats, and large shrimping vessels, packed with Cubans. As the refugees were accepted into the United States, Castro decided to empty the hospitals and prisons, forcing their inhabitants onto boats setting sail for America.

Eventually, the United States could not cope with the numbers of refugees crossing the Straits of Florida and began intercepting and turning back the boats. The policy became that if a boat reached land it would be accepted, but any boats met at sea by the Coast Guard would be rebuffed.

Cuba's government was divided over the émigré situation. The mass exodus decimated Cuba's middle class. Also, dissenters setting up base outside the island created a diaspora that gave voice to those oppressed within Cuba. This kept the world's attention on Castro's internal activities, thus compelling other nations to continue pressuring Castro's regime with sanctions.

The majority of Cuban exiles settled in Miami, Florida, although others moved farther north and created large communities around Union City, New Jersey, and in New York City. Many formed what is termed the Cuban-American lobby, an organization of Cuban refugees who have done much to support and strengthen embargoes by the US government.

Through broadcast programming aimed at Cuba from the United States, such as Radio Martí and TV Martí, Cuban exiles have broadcast both support and propaganda to the resident population, espousing conflicting sets of ideals and still, even though they are settled far from the island's shores, showing solidarity to their brethren.

Since as early as the 19th century, prominent exiles have played a large part

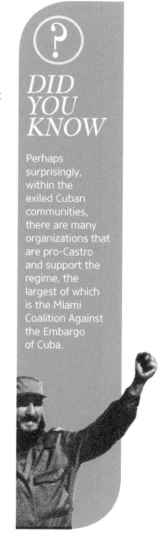

DID YOU KNOW

Perhaps surprisingly, within the exiled Cuban communities, there are many organizations that are pro-Castro and support the regime, the largest of which is the Miami Coalition Against the Embargo of Cuba.

in rallying support for Cuban issues. José Martí was one of the first to base himself in both Spain as well as the United States to raise international support for and awareness of Cuban oppression during the Spanish colonial rule. In the 1950s, even the Castro brothers were originally exiled from prison to Mexico, and they, too, continued to lobby and speak out against the Batista corruption, eventually bringing their cause to the United States. Other prominent Cubans who settled in Europe include the writer Guillermo Cabrera Infante, who escaped to Great Britain, and Carlos Franqui, the poet, writer, and journalist who fled to Italy after opposing Castro's support of Soviet activity in Europe.

In recent years, emigration from Cuba has become easier. The 2012 abolition of the exit permit system has made it easier for Cubans to leave for relocation purposes as well as simply for travel.

THE LAST "ISM"

COLONIALISM, COMMUNISM, NATIONALISM AND . . . TOURISM?

P rior to the socialist revolution of 1959, Cuba was a popular tourist destination. Cuba's climate, scenic beauty, colonial architecture, and expansive beaches, along with its close proximity to other Caribbean islands and the United States, made it a desirable destination for North and South Americans, as well as for Spanish, Portuguese, Italians, and other Europeans.

In the early 20th century, Havana became the most popular destination of any Caribbean city or resort. This was partly helped by an influx of American visitors who were looking to briefly escape Prohibition and easily find access to gambling and entertainment they could not enjoy at home. The influx of American tourists significantly boosted the industry, so behind sugar exports and tobacco, tourism became the third-highest source of Cuban revenue.

With the Great Depression and, later on, World War II contributing to global downturns in the numbers of American and international travelers, Cuba's general tourism industry in the 1950s declined and was replaced by organized crime syndicates that (through casinos) created the "Latin Las Vegas."

The post-revolution embargoes and the eventual travel ban for American citizens caused a rapid decline in tourism in Cuba. The Cuban government's ban on foreign currency, and its outlaw of contact between tourists and locals, all but eradicated tourism. Even before these statutes were imposed, fear for safety had already deterred many non-US nationals from visiting the island, particularly following the Bay of Pigs and Cuban Missile crises.

The collapse of the Soviet Union and the subsequent Special Period that decimated the fragile Cuban economy resulted in the Cuban government taking a renewed interest in tourism as a much-needed source of revenue. Heavy investments were made to restore the dilapidated historic hotels and towns back to pre-revolution standards. However, the plans were designed to create "tourist enclaves," segregating foreign visitors from local people, a policy that became known as "tourism apartheid."

By the late 1990s, despite tourism apartheid, Cuba reaped the benefits of its efforts. Tourists (primarily from Europe and Canada) began to visit the resorts concentrated around Cayo Coco, Holguín, Varadero, and Havana. Soon, tourism was the leading source of revenue for the island, surpassing even export sugar sales.

Travel restrictions for US citizens continued to be problematic, even after Cuba began welcoming foreign visitors. Canada became the largest tourist market for Cuba and, since 2007, the numbers of Canadian visitors has been growing by at least

10 percent each year. As most Canadian arrivals came by charter flights, it's possible that a number of tourists arriving from Canada were in fact US citizens circumventing the restricted travel policies of their own government.

European visitors have also been substantially increasing, particularly tourists from the United Kingdom, Germany, and France, who have competed with the number of guests from Spain and Italy.

In addition, the 1994 reforms of the tourist industry have attracted significant foreign investment in tourist infrastructure, one of the few areas in which Cuba has permitted foreign-held capital. International hotel chains began to operate properties on the island. Also, the improvements made on both airports and docks allowed international air and cruise lines to begin regular transit routes.

The Cuban government put safeguards in place to protect its environment from the influx of foreign visitors. The 1994 creation of a Ministry of Tourism oversaw heavy state investment in and development of tourist facilities. During the 1990's, Cuba invested more than 3.5 billion dollars into tourism, receiving over 10 million visitors.

CUBA VIA CANADA

Unofficial estimates suggest that perhaps 30,000 Americans illegally visit Cuba each year via Canadian travel agencies and flights. Although, Cuba's tourism authorities claim the actual figure is double that.

One of the negative sides of an increase in tourism has been increased prostitution and what is called sex tourism. Castro made it a goal to eliminate prostitution when he came to power, but sex tourism has created a burgeoning black market. Although other nations recognize that Cuba has taken steps to clamp down heavily on child prostitution for foreign visitors, it is still widespread. Further repercussions of the increase in sex tourists include raised rates of sexually transmitted diseases, particularly HIV among the Cuban population.

Although most foreign-owned hotels were opened exclusively for the use of visitors, private houses are now permitted to operate as short-term bed and breakfast accommodations, known as *casas particulares*. The development of this cheaper option of hospitality has had significant benefits for cultural integration between locals and visitors.

In 2008, the enclave system for tourism was abolished, which has opened up tourist facilities to Cubans as well as foreign visitors. Cubans can now stay at hotels in any part of the country they'd like to visit. In practice, however, very few Cubans can afford to take advantage of the opportunity.

Today, more than three million visitors travel to Cuba each year, and tourism has become the biggest source of income for the Cuban economy, outpacing its sugar, tobacco, mineral, and pharmaceutical industries.

Cuba Libre Cocktail

The Cuba Libre cocktail became popular toward the end of the Spanish-American War. The name of the drink translates to "Free Cuba." Although it is similar to a traditional rum and Coke, the addition of lime juice makes this cocktail the lighter option.

SERVES 1 / PREP TIME 3 MINUTES

1. Squeeze the juice from half of a fresh lime into a tumbler glass. Add the ice.
2. Pour 2 ounces of rum into the glass.
3. Add cola to taste and stir well.
4. Add a slice of lime to the rim of the glass. Cheers!

Juice of ½ a fresh lime
Ice cubes, as desired
2 ounces of light rum
Cola
Thick slice of lime

¡ARTISTAS ADELANTE!

ARTS AS POLITICAL EXPRESSION

ollowing the Cuban Revolution and the rise to power of the Castro-led rebels, the new regime established policies for artists within the island that were designed to promote Castro's ideals and stifle expressive dissent. According to Gerardo Mosquera, "a practice of culture as ideological propaganda" was imposed. Castro's own statements questioned the validity of any political expression through art, stating that writers and artists had no right to express any sentiments against the revolution. Not surprisingly, many of the artists and intellectuals began to flee Cuba for the United States. Ironically, while political dissent expressed through artwork was outlawed, the study of art itself began to flourish thanks to the expansion of education programs.

Afro-Cuban art, reflecting the diverse nature of Cuban heritage, was encouraged, largely as part of the drive to reinforce Cuban identity rooted in its historic past. The Grupo Antillano (a group of sculptors, engravers, metal and textile designers, ceramicists, and painters) was encouraged and supported between the mid-1970s and 1980s, and much of their work was exhibited in galleries across the nation.

As Cuba reinvented and continuously promoted nationalism, art was developed and proliferated under careful government scrutiny; only nationalistic expression in favor of the new, post-revolution ideal was allowed.

Younger artists came to the forefront, rebelling against modernism and championing conceptual art, which was based on ideology instead of finished craftsmanship. The New Art movement became the personification of conceptual art and is widely recognized as having its roots within Cuba.

By the 1980s, other groups, such as Volumen Uno, had congregated and were

DID YOU KNOW

The Street Art Movement flourished in Cuba, inspired by Mexican muralist Diego Rivera and engraver José Guadalupe Posada, whose late-19th-century drawings inspired many 20th-century cartoonists.

{ **Nationalism** na·tion·al·ism
A political ideology that involves individuals identifying with and becoming attached to their own nation. }

> **The rebirth of artistic expression** in Cuban art has been largely fueled by new generations of artists born well after the revolution. This burst of young artistry, in all manners of expression, exemplifies the sense of belonging to a modern world without hindrance from previous generations.

highly recognized in the New Art movement. These groups encouraged more politically explicit and engaged work. The tourism of the 1990s gave artists greater opportunity to exhibit and sell their work to the visiting international audience. Counteractive political messaging was not possible in state-controlled galleries.

Throughout post-revolutionary Cuba, political activism other than activism to promote the socialist ideal was prohibited. The only Cuban artists able to incoporate political dissent through their work were those who had escaped abroad.

Raúl Castro has, as with most matters, shown a more moderate tolerance of political debate. The limited Internet access on the island has made it much harder for the government to control and moderate foreign media. Limited blogging has now become more commonplace, and dissenting voices are often heard online. Although official media continues to be highly censored, theater and film have become less restricted.

Performance art has grown but remains highly scrutinized; artists pushing political boundaries are still harshly treated. In December 2014, the graffiti artist El Sexto intended to use two live pigs in his performance, named Fidel and Raúl. He was apprehended and remains in custody.

Another high-profile and recent incident concerned New York–based Cuban Tania Bruguera, who planned to stage an open-mic performance titled *Tatlin's Whisper* at the end of

2014 in Revolution Square. Bruguera was arrested before the performance could begin. Her arrest sparked international condemnation, and many saw it as a reminder of the limits of expression that still exist.

According to a January 2015 *New York Times* article by Victoria Burnett, the problem for the Cuban government is often not necessarily what is being expressed through art, but rather where it is being expressed. Rubén del Valle Lantarón, president of the National Council of Visual Arts, offered Bruguera other venues in which to perform, which she rejected. In part, the objection from the authorities was that the performance would take place on "hallowed ground" in Revolution Square, whereas Bruguera's counterargument was that the alternatives offered could be restricted for all those who might want to participate. The stalemate has not yet eased.

This incident is a recent example of artistic freedom being tested in Cuba. The lines between art and politics remain blurred. In other artistic fields, particularly in popular music, tolerance has grown for styles previously spurned as subversive. Rap and hip-hop were both rejected by Cuban authorities as they grew in popularity across North America. Seen as a musical expression of capitalism and too closely tied to American culture, the genre only began to gain acceptance once young Cubans injected their own energy into the music and lyrics. Now the government tacitly approves of both genres as a route to the hearts and minds of the younger generation of Cubans.

RUMBA, SALSA, & REGGAETON

MUSIC THAT HAS DEFINED CUBAN CULTURE

Cuban music has been hugely influential worldwide and has been described as one of the most popular forms of regional music since recording began. The rumba, salsa, jazz, and dubstep genres all owe a debt to the influence of Cuban music.

Cuban rumba grew from Cuba's Spanish and African heritage. It includes dance, percussion, and song. The name rumba originally comes from the word "party." Enslaved Africans working the sugar plantations created the drumming and dance rhythm of rumba in order to preserve their heritage during slavery.

Although salsa's roots can be traced to the music of Cuba's mambo and guaracha genres, it is generally regarded as a fusion of Cuban, Puerto Rican, and Colombian dance music. The name salsa was first crafted in New York in the 1970s, largely from the Cuban dance-style music that had been popular since the 1940s.

Cubatón—the unique form of Cuban reggaeton—was popularized in the early 21st century. Reggaeton's root is Jamaican reggae, but as the style developed across Latin America, other musical influences, such as hip-hop, permeated this music. Cubatón is the expression of reggaeton most commonly heard in Cuba, although critics are divided over whether it should be regarded as a separate genre in itself.

While the Cuban government has been tolerant of salsa, rumba, and more recently, hip-hop, it has reacted harshly to the proliferation of reggaeton music, denouncing it as degenerate. While authorities have not banned it from being played on radio, they have demanded that it be played minimally.

Reggaeton can also claim roots in salsa, but the dance moves can be seen as more sensual, involving the rhythmic movements of the hips. Salsa is far quicker and can be incorporated into line (or circle) dancing in groups. It is generally a party dance for all to celebrate. Still, rumba dancing tends to be the easiest to master as the steps mainly involve footwork alternating between left and right.

OBAMA & THE FUTURE OF CUBA

WHAT CAN NORMALIZATION MEAN?

The most recent period of Cuban history, after the retirement of Fidel Castro and the succession of his brother Raúl, has become known as the Cuban Thaw, a term coined by international media to describe the warming of relations between the island and its largest neighbor, the United States. The 2008 election of Barack Obama to the US presidency brought new hope to Cubans (those in exile and within the island) that a new path to normalization could be found. As of December 2014, major steps were taken to continue the thaw.

The election of Pope Francis as the leader of the Catholic Church and the Vatican City State in 2013 proved influential in

Cuban-American relations. Covertly, Pope Francis attended discussions between Cuba and the United States, both in Canada and at the Vatican. Following these secret meetings, on December 17, 2014, the two presidents announced the start of a process to normalize their countries' relationship. The agreement immediately relaxed financial and travel restrictions, and prioritized the reestablishment of embassies and diplomatic relations.

Following the announcement, a prisoner exchange took place, and in January 2015, 53 Cuban dissidents were released from prison in Cuba, some of whom had been held in jails for 20 years.

As part of the December 2014 agreements, President Obama signed an executive order to facilitate the export and import of goods between the two nations while also easing travel restrictions for Americans. The order was signed on January 16, 2015, granting travel licenses and limited trade support to the burgeoning private sector within Cuba. However, an act of Congress is still needed to end the standing trade embargo.

The impact on Cuban society and its standing in the wider world has been positively received. In 2013, Raúl Castro

EARLY ADOPTERS

The entertainment industry immediately capitalized on the softened relations, making it possible for Conan O'Brien to film his late-night talk show on the island in February 2015. Major League Baseball began exploring the possibility of spring training taking place in Cuba in 2016.

stated that the process of a "slow and orderly transfer of the leadership of the revolution to the new generations" had begun and that he privately pledged to retire in 2018 after 10 years of presidency.

Castro championed the future benefits that improved relations with the United States would bring to Cuba, while extolling the progress of the revolution that had brought him and his brother to power decades earlier. He also highlighted the economic benefits possible from lifting the Cuban embargo.

The international reactions to the announcements made by Obama and Castro have been generally positive.

In January of 2015, former President Fidel Castro made a rare statement, through a carefully worded announcement featured on the front page of *Granma* (the official newspaper of the central committee of the Cuban Communist Party). Although Castro wrote that he did not "trust the policy of the United States," he noted somewhat more diplomatically that "we will always defend cooperation and friendship with all the peoples of the world, among them our political adversaries."

The international reactions to the announcements made by presidents Obama and Castro have been generally positive. The Canadian foreign affairs minister, John Baird, claimed that the process of normalization could transform Cuba for the better.

Even nations normally critical of the government praised the process. Venezuelan President Nicolás Maduro was particularly fulsome in his comments regarding President Obama, despite the usually critical tone of their relationship.

Within the United States, political reaction has been extremely mixed. Outspoken critics from both Democrat and Republican sides have voiced concerns. Democratic Senator Bob Menendez—himself a Cuban-American—was particularly vocal in his opposition to the moves. Republican senators Rand Paul and Jeff Flake have, on the other hand, been largely supportive, even criticizing their colleague, Florida Senator Marco Rubio, for his opposition to the accord.

Whether or not the thaw will continue following the next presidential election is not clear. Front-runners for the post have yet to fully emerge, although former secretary of state Hillary Clinton, arguably the leading Democratic candidate, has strongly endorsed all moves to normalize relations between the two countries.

Today, US visitors to Cuba can bring home up to $100 of alcohol and tobacco and $400 in total goods, which are for the first time available for purchase with credit cards. Banking transactions now are permitted as companies are allowed to open accounts in each nation.

After nearly 60 years of isolation from its former ally, it would seem that Cuba, tenuously but surely, is on its way to full reconciliation with the United States.

A PARTING
THOUGHT

"Man loves liberty, even if he does not know that he loves it.
He is driven by it and flees from where it does not exist."

—JOSÉ MARTÍ, CUBAN NATIONAL HERO

BIBLIOGRAPHY

2010 Observatory of Economic Complexity

Anderson, John Lee. *Che Guevara—A Revolutionary Life.*
New York: Grove Press, 2010.

Associated Press Archives—*Official History of U.S. Navy Base.*

Batista, Fulgencio. *The Growth and Decline of the Cuban Republic.* New York:
Devin-Adair Publishing Company, 1964.

Bourne, Peter. *Fidel. A Biography of Fidel Castro.* New York: Dodd, Mead & Co, 1986.

Franklin, Jane. *Cuba and the United States: A Chronological History.* North
Melbourne, Australia: Ocean Press, 2002.

Gott, Richard. *Cuba—A New History.* New Haven, CT: Yale University Press, 2005.

Kellner, Douglas. *Ernesto "Che" Guevara.* New York: Chelsea House
Publishers, 1989.

Navarro, José Cantón. *History of Cuba.* SI-MAR, 2001.

Sweig, Julia E. *Inside the Cuban Revolution.* Cambridge, MA: Harvard University
Press, 2004.

Thomas, Hugh. *Cuba—The Pursuit of Freedom.* Boston: Da Capo Press, 1998.

US State Department: *A guide to the United States' History of recognition,
diplomatic and consular relations by country since 1776: Cuba.*

www.bbc.com

www.benzinga.com

www.cnn.com

www.cubahistory.org

www.sfgate.com

www.georgetown.edu

www.historyofcuba.com

www.nationsonline.org

www.nytimes.com

www.pbs.org

INDEX

CONTINUE THE
CONVERSATION

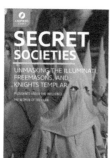

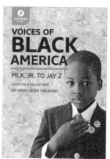

CPSIA information can be obtained at www.ICGtesting.com
Printed in the USA
BVOW11s1114290515

402313BV00004B/4/P

9 781942 411314